The TEMPLE

The TEMPLE

Where Heaven Meets Earth

Truman G. Madsen

DESERET
BOOK

SALT LAKE CITY, UTAH

Text © 2008 Truman G. Madsen

Library of Congress Cataloging-in-Publication Data

Madsen, Truman G.
  The temple : where heaven meets earth / Truman G. Madsen.
      p. cm.
  Includes bibliographical references and index.
  ISBN 978-1-59038-926-3 (hardcover : alk. paper)
  1. Mormon temples. 2. Temples. I. Title.
  BX8643.T4M33 2008
  246'.95893—dc22   2008016072

Printed in the United States of America
Worzalla Publishing Co., Stevens Point, WI

10 9 8 7 6 5 4 3 2 1

CONTENTS

PREFACE

For decades, whatever else I have studied or written, I have been motivated to explore vital temple purposes, preoccupied with their origins and applications.

Much that I have learned in this quest is in and between the lines of these chapters.

As a personal manifesto, let me submit four preludes.

First, I remember a turbulent storm one dark night. On the horizon, light penetrated the almost blinding clouds. We could make out, even at a distance, the illumined spires of the Manti Temple.

"You know," said the temple president, "that temple is never more beautiful than during a storm."

So it is with all temples that now extend into every hemisphere.

I have come to know the kinds of storms, both subtle and violent, that we all sooner or later face in this world. I have come to

know the beauties—which include truths and powers and blessings and promises—inside temples that cannot be fully conferred
and embraced by covenants anywhere else on the planet.

I have come to know the wisdom of one of my longtime
friends who said to me in a solemn setting—almost his last
words—"All the Lord's answers are in the temple."

He meant answers to daily perplexities—spiritual and temporal. In the temple they merge.

He meant guiding and comforting answers that come directly
from on high amidst sacred silence.

He meant also the temple's peace-giving sustenance, which
undergirds the most far-reaching concerns of life, what Hugh
Nibley called "getting one's bearings on the universe." These are
questings that "stretch to the utmost heavens."

In my own life and that of my family through five generations, I have witnessed and verified these godly influences.

Second, a time ago, we pulled a consortium of experts
together. They were focused on Jewish temple lore, and on Jesus
and the temple.

Their mastery of biblical and extrabiblical sources gave us new
appreciation for ancient and modern sanctuaries. "If you want to
know why the Latter-day Saints build temples," said Frank Cross,
who is well-known for his studies of the Dead Sea Scrolls, "read
the Bible."

Ours is the privilege to know firsthand. Modern temples
restore and transcend the communion of earlier sanctuaries. They
require us to bring to the altar what is deepest inside us in the
spirit of consecration.

Third, we learned of a rabbi who undertook to find the earliest roots in Chaldean and Hebrew of the word we translate "joy."

It led him to the word *avodah,* which translates as "works" or "service." It refers to the sacrificial ritual of the day of atonement. His book concludes that in antiquity among the Israelites, the most joyous service was temple service.

My cumulative experience and that of my associates demonstrates that there is such resilient joy. The temple is the place where Christ's atonement manifests to us the "peaceable things—that which bringeth joy, that which bringeth life eternal" (D&C 42:61).

To miss the joy is to miss the point.

Fourth, it is recognized today that DNA determines multiple traits and dispositions of our bodily makeup. It places an unerasable identification tag on every cell. In this sense we not only *have* forebears, but we *are* our forebears.

If we are bold enough, and we are encouraged to be (for from baptism to sealing, the idea of birth and rebirth is the presupposition of every ordinance), we may reverently trace our pedigree beyond the veil and rediscover our celestial parentage.

The intent of the heavens in temples is to extend celestial parenting to our bodies.

The same God who commanded that "Holiness to the Lord" be inscribed on every eastward spire and on every doorknob invites us to be inscribed with his name in every part of our being. His envisioned outcome is that we become as he is: living temples.

In a world that is in crucial need of regeneration, I know firsthand that this process is underway.

It has been said that in the life to come, "There is only one sorrow, not to be a saint."

In contrast there can be supernal joy—in us and in the Father and the Son—for those who have been saintly enough to extend the everlasting influences of the temple to those who come before and after us. For we will open up for them, as for ourselves, creative possibilities in worlds without end.

In sum, I am among the number who know that Christ is the way, the truth, and the life. And his way, his truth, his life are most indelibly infused into our souls in his house, the House of the Lord.

These writings have been available in other compilations, and on web sites. But whether in or out of print, some are hard to find. I have been asked, "Why not bring these chapters together in one place?"

(Apparently many of us are at ease with computer-eze. Yet at times we would rather turn a page than scroll a screen.)

So here in book form are the combined chapters. There is necessarily some repetition, but it has been reduced to a minimum.

Clearly I have not written officially but only as a "layman enthralled."

But if these studies can help readers, anywhere and in anyway, to enhance their temple experience, in the image of the Redeemer, I will be more than grateful.

1

HOUSE OF GLORY

I begin with a story that goes back before the dedication of the Salt Lake Temple, which took forty years to build. President David O. McKay used to tell of a man who didn't have money enough even to buy shoes to attend a conference in the Tabernacle. During the conference Brigham Young arose and pleaded with the brethren that there needed to be more granite brought for the temple from the quarry about fifteen miles south. It was hauled mostly by ox team. A man came out from this conference and saw another man on the street with a team of oxen. "Why weren't you in there, Brother?"

"Uh, my feet. I didn't feel right about going in."

"Well, Brother Brigham pleaded for more people to get granite."

"All right," said the man, "I'll go. Wo, hah, Buck!" And he started.[1] President McKay's eyes filled with tears as he related that simple incident. The reason why his name and his image come to mind whenever I think of temples is that it was President McKay who performed the wedding ceremony for my wife, Ann, and myself, and that high privilege was possible for us in part because he had done the same for Ann's parents. That morning, very early on a June day, he came in his white suit, a white tie, and white hair. There was majesty in his personality. Somehow we knew then, had we ever doubted it, that no one could speak properly if he spoke evil of the temple, for there before us stood its product.

John the Revelator, John the Beloved, envisioning the city Jerusalem in glorified state, said, "And I saw no temple therein: for the Lord God Almighty and the Lamb are the temple of it" (Revelation 21:22). And then he added that not only would the Lamb reign forever, as we sing, but we, having by then been glorified like unto Him, would likewise reign forever and ever (see Revelation 22:5).

The Salt Lake Temple was dedicated with a sense of sacrifice and gratitude that maybe we moderns have not reached. Forty years! Forty thousand people gathered just to see the laying of the capstone! And Lorenzo Snow, then one of the Twelve, led them in the Hosanna Shout. And then Wilford Woodruff, who had had a dream years before that he would somehow be involved in the dedication of that temple (and he was by now the President of the Church), promised that a strict reading of the requirements of worthiness would not be imposed on the members attending the dedicatory services provided they came feasting and repenting. (That was not a slip of the lip, because the Lord defines fasting and prayer in modern revelation—granting it has its negative side of mourning in some places—as rejoicing and prayer [see D&C 59:13–14]. Fasting is feasting on the Spirit, and somehow not partaking of physical food isn't quite enough. Fasting is a kind of concentration, a kind of pulling ourselves together.)

During a twenty-three-day period of dedicatory services averaging two thousand people each session, some eighty thousand were regenerated. President Woodruff's entry in his journal at the end of that year was: "The greatest event of the year [1893] is the dedication of the Salt Lake Temple. Great power was manifest on that occasion."[2] The scriptural phrase that brings all that into a theme is that we are to receive in temples, through temples, from temples, "power from on high" (D&C 95:8). Christ is the source of that power. The temple is His. Every symbol in and out of that sacred structure points toward Him and, as a cup carries water, transmits the Holy Spirit.

Now let me be specific in terms of needs that all of us feel strongly about in our time. It is a characteristic fact that the Lord has commanded the sacrifice of temple building at the times when apparently our people were least able to build them; and the sacrifice has been immense. But sacrifice brings forth blessings.

In the 1830s the Brethren kept inquiring. They didn't have our heritage, and they didn't understand even what the word *temple* meant. They kept asking, What is it we are doing? Well, we build a temple. What for? And Joseph Smith told them on one occasion, "The endowment you are so anxious about, you cannot comprehend now, nor could Gabriel explain it to [your] understanding." But prepare, he told them, for great blessings will come.[3] Yet in a preparatory revelation (see D&C 88) the purposes of the temple are outlined. It's called "a house of prayer, a house of fasting, a house of faith, a house of learning, a house of glory, . . . a house of God" (D&C 88:119). Prepare yourselves, it says; "sanctify yourselves . . . and [God] will unveil his face unto you" (D&C 88:68).

Let's discuss each of those purposes.

A house of prayer. "Make yourselves acquainted," said the

Prophet, "with those men who like Daniel pray three times a day toward the House of the Lord."[4] There is a true principle involved in literally facing the house of God as one prays and as one praises the Lord. The Prophet, as he met with a group of faithful Saints prior to the completion of the Nauvoo Temple (he did not live to see that day), said to them, "[You do] not know how to pray to have your prayers answered." But, as the sister who recorded that brief statement testifies, she and her husband received their temple blessings, and then came to understand what he meant.[5] A modern Apostle, Elder Melvin J. Ballard, said once to a group of young people about solving their problems: "Study it out in your own minds, reach a conclusion, and then go to the Lord with it and he will give you an answer by that inward burning, and if you don't get your answer I will tell you where to go—go to the house of the Lord. Go with your hearts full of desire to do your duty. When in the sacred walls of these buildings, where you are entitled to the Spirit of the Lord, and in the silent moments, the answer will come."[6]

For clues to personal experiences behind that statement we note that in Elder Ballard's boyhood he often looked up at the Logan Temple and its spires, was inspired by those spires, and wanted to enter the temple worthily regardless of the costs. That meant, for one thing, that he never even entertained the temptation to break the Word of Wisdom, because he knew that might prevent him from entering that building. His later experiences, many having to do with his ministry, were often a derivative of what he felt and experienced within the walls of the sanctuary.

On a personal note, I myself, in a critical year away from home and at school, drove at times to the place in Los Angeles where we had been told there would one day be a temple, just in the feeling that the place might be an added strength to me in prayer. And it proved to be so.

"A house of prayer, a house of fasting, a house of faith, a house of learning." One of the men who touched my life was Elder John A. Widtsoe of the Council of the Twelve, a man who graduated *summa cum laude* from Harvard after three instead of the usual four years, who was given in that last year an award for the greatest depth of specializing in his field (which was soil chemistry); but they also gave an award that year for the student who had shown the greatest breadth of interests, which he also received. Elder Widtsoe wrote perceptively about the temple and temple worship. I heard him say in sacred circumstances that the promise was given him by a patriarch when he was a mere boy in Norway, "Thou shalt have great faith in the ordinances of the Lord's House." And so he did. I heard him say that the temple is so freighted with depth of understanding, so loaded with symbolic grasp of life and its eternal significance, that only a fool would attempt in mere prosaic restatement to explain it in a comprehensive way.

I heard him say that the temple is a place of revelation. And he did not divorce that concept from the recognition that the problems we have are very practical, very realistic, down-to-earth problems. He often said, "I would rather take my practical problems to the house of the Lord than anywhere else." In his book *In a Sunlit Land* he describes a day when, having been frustrated for months in trying to pull together a mass of data he had compiled to come up with a formula, he took his companion, his wife, to the Logan Temple to forget his failure. And in one of the rooms of that structure there came, in light, the very answer he had previously failed to find.[7] Two books on agrarian chemistry grew out of that single insight—a revelation in the temple of God.

The temple is not just a union of heaven and earth. It is the key to our mastery of the earth. It is the Lord's graduate course in subduing the earth, which, as only Latter-day Saints understand, ultimately will be heaven—this earth glorified.

A house of learning? Yes, and we learn more than about the earth. We learn *ourselves*. We come to comprehend more deeply, in an environment that surrounds us like a cloak, our own identity, something of the roots that we can't quite reach through memory but which nevertheless are built cumulatively into our deepest selves—an infinite memory of conditions that predate memory. The temple is the catalyst whereby the self is revealed to the self.

There was a period when I was required as an officer in the Ensign Stake to go every Friday to the temple. It was not a burden, as I had thought it would be. It became instead my joy. Slowly, because of that regularity, I was trusted with certain assignments in the temple. I had the privilege to sit for hours in the chapel of the annex or elsewhere, contemplative, reading occasionally, but trying to absorb, trying to breathe the air that is heavier than air in that place. There I would meditate about my critical problems, which had to do with decisions about my life's work, decisions about the girl I should marry, and other struggles in how to cope. There were times when I learned something about me; there were times when peace came in a decision, and I knew that that peace was of God.

The temple is a house of learning. And it is intended that therein we not simply learn *of* or *about* Christ, but that we come to *know Him*. It has always impressed me that in the Joseph Smith Translation the classic passage about the hereafter when many will say, "Lord, Lord, did we not do this and that?" is rendered more fittingly. The King James Version says that Christ will respond, "I never knew you." The Joseph Smith Translation renders it, "You never knew me" (Matthew 7:23; JST, Matthew 7:33).

This is the gospel of Jesus Christ. This is the restored Church of Jesus Christ. This is the church that teaches us that we can have a direct and immediate living relationship with the living Christ. And we inscribe on temples, "Holiness to the Lord. The House of the Lord." He told us, and He didn't qualify it, that as regards our preparation, "all the pure in heart that come into it shall see God" (D&C 97:16). Elder Orson Pratt pointed out that this promise specifically relates to a temple not yet built, a temple to be erected in the center city, the New Jerusalem, wherein someday Christ actually will dwell and wherein, therefore, any who enter will meet Him.[8] But again, Elders John A. Widtsoe, George F. Richards, Joseph Fielding Smith, and others have borne witness that the promise is more extensive than that, that it applies now.[9] It is a promise that we may have a wonderfully rich communion with Him. Communion! That is to say that we are not simply learning propositions about, but that we are in a participative awareness with.

Occasionally we struggle in amateur research in Church history to understand what kind of a portrait, in terms of sheer physical appearance, we could draw of Christ if we simply utilized what modern witnesses have said about their glimpses of Him. It's an impressive portrait. But one thing perhaps we sometimes neglect in that curiosity is an awareness, or a seeking for an awareness, of His personality, of those subtler realities that we already recognize in other persons in all variations but which have been perfected in Him. What would it be like to be in His presence, not simply in terms of what you would see but what you would feel? To give us one clue, He says, "Listen to him . . . who is pleading your cause before [the Father]—saying: Father, behold the sufferings and death of him who did no sin [that is to say, committed none, but he knows sins, for he experienced temptation to do them all], in whom thou wast well pleased; behold the blood of thy Son which was shed . . . ; wherefore, Father, spare these my brethren" (D&C 45:3–5). That's a glimpse of the compassion that one comes to feel in communion—the feeling with, the feeling for, that He has. He is the one personality of whom it cannot truthfully be said, "You don't know me. You don't understand me. You don't care about me." Because of what He went through, He does know, He does understand, He does care. And He has had us sacrifice to build sacred houses where the linkage of His heart, His "bowels of compassion," can merge with ours.

The temple is a place of learning to know Him.

And now the phrase "a house of glory, a house of God." One of the most tender moments of my spiritual life was the day that Rose Wallace Bennett, an author I knew, told me that as a little girl she was present in the dedicatory services of the Salt Lake Temple. She described also the day Wilford Woodruff had a birthday, his ninetieth, when some eight thousand children between the ages of eight and twelve, all dressed in white, were in the Tabernacle and a little girl took ninety roses forward to him. They had gathered to honor him; and then as he had come into the building (under some pretense that there was need of an organ repair), they arose and sang "We Thank Thee, O God, for a Prophet." She could not talk about what it felt like to see his tears, or again, what it was like to be in the temple, without herself weeping. But what she said to me was, "Young man, my father brought me to the edge of City Creek Canyon where we could look down on the temple. I testify to you that there was a light around the temple, and it was not due to electricity."

There are such phrases in all the authentic literature that has to do with temple dedications: "light," "glory," "power." Even some who were not members of the Church at Kirtland came running, wondering what had happened. They wondered if the building was on fire. It was—but with what the Prophet called "celestial burnings," the downflow of the power of the living God, like encircling flame as on the day of Pentecost. A prayer for that had been offered by the Prophet and by his father, and it was fulfilled (see D&C 109:36–37).[10]

What is glory? It is many things in the scriptures. One strand of meaning is often neglected. If we can trust one Hebrew student, the Hebrew word equivalent to glory, *kabod,* refers in some of its strands to physical presence. Just as a person says in common parlance today, "He was there in all his glory," so the Old Testament often uses this word for God. In a psalm that refers to glory (Psalm 8) there are two changes that are crucial. The King James Version reads, "Thou hast made [man] a little lower than the angels, and hast crowned him with glory and honour." Probably what that verse said originally was, "Thou hast made [man] a little lower than the Gods, and hath crowned him with a *physical body* and with honor." This is the truth. The body is a step *up* in the scale of progression, not a step down. God is God because He is gloriously embodied; and were He not so embodied, He would be less than God.

The privilege of attending the house of God is in effect to have our physical beings brought into harmony with our spirit personalities. And I have read, but cannot quote perfectly, can only paraphrase, the testimony of President Lorenzo Snow to the effect that participating in the temple ceremonies is the only way that the knowledge locked in one's spirit can become part of this flesh; thus occurs that inseparable union, that blending, which makes possible a celestial resurrection. It is as if, if I may mix the figure, we are given in the house of God a patriarchal blessing to every organ and attribute and power of our being, a blessing that is to be fulfilled in this world and the next, keys and insights that can enable us to live a godly life in a very worldly world, protected—yes, even insulated—from the poisons and distortions that are everywhere.

That is the temple. And the glory of God, His ultimate perfection, is in His house duplicated in us, provided we go there with a susceptible attitude.

Let me briefly discuss the "how" of susceptibility. Listening once in Los Angeles to the plea of President David O. McKay, stake president after stake president pledged contributions to make possible the building of the Los Angeles Temple. They made a commitment. Then he arose and delivered a masterful discourse, maybe the greatest I have ever heard on the subject of temples. In shorthand I jotted down one paragraph which I'm going to quote, but before I do so, let me give this explanation. He told of a girl— a girl, I found out later, who was his niece and therefore felt confident in confiding in him. Earlier that year she had been initiated into a sorority, and not long thereafter she had "gone through the temple" (as we say); I wish that verb could be improved—"going through the temple." I wish we could somehow speak of the temple going through *us*. I wish that my children had not been confused—it's my fault that they were—when my wife and I used to say to them, "We are going to *do* sealings." They thought that we would take a stepladder and a bucket. It's a kind of Mormon activism to talk about "temple work." There is a sense, of course, in which it is work; but too rarely do we speak of "temple worship," which can send us back to our work changed.

On this occasion in Los Angeles, President McKay stopped everyone by saying: "This young lady came to me. She had had both experiences, but said she had been far more impressed with her sorority." We gasped.

President McKay was a master of the pause. He let that wait for several seconds and then said: "Brothers and sisters, she was disappointed in the temple. Brothers and sisters, I was disappointed in the temple." Then he finished his sentence: "And so were you." Then no one gasped. He had us.

"*Why* were we?" he asked. And then he named some of the things. We were not prepared. How could we be, fully? We had stereotypes in our minds, faulty expectations. We were unable to distinguish the symbol from the symbolized. We were not worthy enough. We were too inclined quickly to respond negatively, critically. And we had not yet seasoned spiritually. Those are my words, but they cover approximately what he said. I will give you the quotation verbatim.

This was a man, at that time eighty years of age, who had been in the temple every week for some fifty years, which gave him, I thought, some right to speak. He said: "I believe there are few, even temple workers, who comprehend the full meaning and power of the temple endowment. Seen for what it is, it is the step-by-step ascent into the Eternal Presence. If our young people could but glimpse it, it would be the most powerful spiritual motivation of their lives."

When he said that, I felt it. I had myself been a critic, had made up my mind that some things were trivial, offensive. But that day the Lord touched me, and I decided that I would not speak again against the house of the Lord. I would not assume I knew better than the prophets. I would listen. And I would repent. And I would hope that someday I could testify as did that noble man. In time there was far more opened up to me than I had ever dreamed.

But there were three things amiss in me, and I dare to suppose these may apply to some others. First, I hadn't even carefully read the scriptures about the temple. It had not occurred to me that there are over three hundred verses, by my count, in the Doctrine and Covenants alone that talk about the temple and the "hows," if you will, of preparation. I had not read what the Brethren had said to help us—I was unaware of those statements. Today we are well supplied with informative material in books such as *The House of the Lord* by Elder James E. Talmage, *The Holy Temple* by Elder Boyd K. Packer, many articles in the *Ensign* and other Church magazines; and several articles in the *Encyclopedia of Mormonism,* volume 4.

Second, I was, I am afraid, afflicted with various kinds of unworthiness and not too anxious to change all that. Oh, we talk of it and we aspire. We want change, but we don't want it enough. We are (and I don't laugh at poor Augustine for saying this) like Augustine, who said in a prayer, "Oh, God, make me clean, but not yet." We talk of sacrifice. The one the Lord asks of us *now* is the sacrifice of our sins—the hardest thing in the world to give up. There's still a certain bittersweet enjoyment. But His promise is crystal clear: "If you will purify yourselves, sanctify yourselves, I will bless you" (see D&C 88:74). And I'm afraid the postscript is: "And if you don't, I can't."

The third point is that I had a built-in hostility to ritual and to symbolism. I was taught by people both in and out of the Church—with good intention, I have no doubt—that we don't believe in pagan ceremony; we don't believe in all these procedures and routines; that's what they did in the ancient apostate church; we've outgrown all that. That in effect is throwing out the baby with the bath water. We're not against ordinances. God has revealed them anew. And I suspect they are as eternal as are what we often call eternal laws. There are certain patterns or programs, certain chains of transmission, which are eternal. Ordinances tie in with those, if they are not identical with them. God has so decreed, but that decree is based upon the very ultimate nature of reality. You *cannot* receive the powers of godliness, says the scripture, except through the ordinances (see D&C 84:20). That hadn't ever entered my soul. I thought our sacraments were a bit of an embarrassment and that sometime we could do away with them. One day it suddenly became clear to me—this is the Lord's pattern of our nourishment. We need spiritual transformation. We can eat, if you will, receive, drink (the Lord uses all those images) the Living Fountain through ordinances. I pray that we will reach out for what is written, reach out for repentance, and reach out in the recognition that the ordinances are channels of living power.

The dedicatory prayers for temples have from the beginning been given by revelation, and that fact has been puzzling to some. How can the Lord reveal a prayer to offer to Him who has revealed it? There's nothing contradictory in that. One cannot know fully what to pray until he receives guidance from the Lord. "He that asketh in the Spirit," says modern revelation, "asketh according to the will of God" (D&C 46:30). You must listen in order to know what to say. And prayers that are all ask and no listen lack something in effectiveness.

The temple is the place where we can come to understand what the Lord would have us ask. And it is the place where we can ask in silence, in joy, in earnestness.

Years ago I was involved in the Ensign Stake genealogical committee. We held a series of firesides. The climactic one of six, on temple marriage, was given by President Joseph Fielding Smith. But the week before that I had been asked to speak on vital temple purposes. I struggled with that. I was talking to young people.

What was most remarkable came toward the end of what I said. I wanted somehow to let them know that my own assurance about marriage had come within the walls of the temple.

But I didn't want to acknowledge publicly that I was going to marry this girl. That had not yet been said in private, and therefore I didn't think it should be said in public. But there came down on me that night (and I have a tape recording that tells the story) such a witness that I announced, "The Lord has made known to me that I am to be married, and to whom." She was on the front row, sitting next to my father. It came as a bit of a surprise to him, too. There was much salt water spilled. Have you heard Pasternak's phrase, "Be so close to those you love that when they weep you taste salt"? I did. I gasped, though, at what I had said and wanted somehow to alter, qualify, call back, change. That was shown in several seconds of silence. Then at last all I could do was say, "In the name of the Lord, amen," and sit down.

For all of us there is something about the temple that can change our lives. We need to reach for it, to honor it, if need be to sacrifice for it, sacrificing even our sins. Some of us have fought against that, as I fought against it, because it means change, maybe some painful change. But that change is the Spirit of God working on the soul, and it will come to each one of us. We will honor the promptings and let the Lord take over in our lives.

The Lord *is* in His temples, where He ministers personally and manifests Himself to the faithful therein. With the power of Christ in His sanctuary, it is intended that all of us drink deeply, receive powerfully, and then testify worthily of that glorious truth. In this way we will come to share in the joys and blessings of the radiant life.

2

FOUNDATIONS OF
TEMPLE WORSHIP

This chapter grows out of fifty years' experience in participating in temple worship, but also from interviewing literally thousands of people for temple recommends and from conversation about their experiences. I hope these words will sink more deeply into you than ever and motivate you to focus your lives on temple worship and on the power of Jesus Christ, which is there. So I'm going to give you an acronym, a few ABCs, and use each of those letters as a lead-in, a memory peg.

Let's begin, then, with *A,* which, in temple focus, may mean both Atonement and anointing. I have learned in the Holy Land that those two words are almost synonymous in Hebrew. The word *kippur,* which is the word for atoning, or atoning influence, means, among other things, "to smear," literally, as in anointing with oil. But it also means to cover, and in awareness of Christ that means to overcome and heal, to cover up and replace sin in our lives with light and healing. The ancient high priest went into the temple only once a year, on the Day of Atonement, Yom Kippur, and the idea was that he would cleanse the temple and, in that very process, cleanse the people, unless, peradventure, they were beyond repentance.

We have been taught by modern revelation that Christ is Himself the Great High Priest. When He promises that He will place His name and His seal and His glory upon His sanctuary, then all who enter therein must come as worthily as they can and leave even worthier. He is the power of repentance, and all the first principles are manifest in the temple: faith, repentance, baptism, and the power of the Holy Ghost.

The next letter is *B,* and I suggest the words *born* or *born again.* Today the religious world often speaks of the "twice-born person," or of being a "born-again Christian," not fully comprehending how complete is His promise to those who come to Him. It is one thing to have faith and another to have repentance, but in the house of the Lord, His house, He requires of His children a covenant making from the heart. And then He makes promises even more inclusive than those that come with the first principles and ordinances. When the Prophet Joseph Smith sent the first Twelve abroad to Britain, one of the instructions he gave is summed up in one sentence. He said, "Being born again, comes by the Spirit of God through ordinances."[1] And all ordinances, therefore, are channels of His Spirit. But the crowning ordinances are those of the holy temple. "Being born again, comes by the Spirit of God through ordinances."

Let's go to *C,* for covenants. The temple is a house of covenant making. I recall in my own earlier days, just before my mission, when I began to understand how deep-reaching and far-reaching these covenants are; I remember shrinking in a way, inwardly, and saying, "I'm not ready; I'm not ready to make that kind of promise." I am now convinced that the sooner you can give your whole heart to covenant making, the greater can be your expectations of the Lord's blessings. I believe that as long as we say, sometimes dishonestly, "Well, I don't want to make a promise like that; I'm afraid I couldn't keep it," we're only beginning to get ready to think about anticipating, and that does not bring any strength.

It's when you make a covenant, and mean it, in the presence of witnesses, and even in the sense of the presence of God, that the heavens begin to shake for your good. And then He promises, "I make the same covenant with you, and I will never break it." Ultimately He asks us to give our all in covenant making, with the promise that then, and only then, He will give His all in our behalf. As we live in righteousness, every blessing that is possible to receive will come to us in greater and greater fulfillment. The everlasting covenant, the new and everlasting covenant, centers in His sanctuary, the temple.

So we move to *D*, dedication. Many of us have been (or will be) privileged to attend a temple dedication. There a prophet of God exercises keys of the priesthood. He alone exercises all the keys of the holy priesthood, including the keys that we understand were given in the Kirtland Temple: the keys of Elijah; keys that involve the blessings of Abraham, Isaac, and Jacob; keys that have to do with the eventual fulfillment of the patriarchal order of the priesthood. It is often said that in the process of dedicating a structure the hope is that we will dedicate ourselves and that thereafter we will be living temples. Modern revelation says that the elements, your elements, the very elements of your spirit and body, are the tabernacle of God, even temples (see D&C 93:33–35). Although we could betray that sacredness (we can defile the temple), it is in the house of the Lord that we gain power to fulfill the promise that we can become living temples like unto Him.

It interests me that no covenant is ever required of us that isn't immediately followed by a divine blessing to further enable us to keep it. So if we are baptized, we receive the promise of the Holy Ghost. If we partake of the sacrament, we are promised the Spirit will be with us, even always (see Moroni 4:3). And in the house of the Lord, we likewise are promised an endowment of power, equivalent to the consecration of our own efforts in keeping our covenants.

Which leads us, then, to *E*, endowment. The Lord has said, "You shall be endowed with power from on high" (D&C 38:32; see 124:40–41), defined in another revelation as the very "power of godliness" (see D&C 84:20–21). How can I live a godly life in this life with all of the struggles that pertain to it? Answer: If I am a recipient of an increased endowment of the Spirit of God. And how does He define the "powers of godliness"? I connect the passage to another in the Doctrine and Covenants that says that we can become possessors (listen to this), possessors of all things. And then it names four specific things: "the life and the light, the Spirit and the power, sent forth by the will of the Father through Jesus Christ, his Son" (D&C 50:27). I suggest to you, out of my own experience, that the temple experience can be enlivening, enlightening, vitalizing, and empowering, and that we need to go back and back to have that experience.

What's next? The word for *F*, recurrent in the Doctrine and Covenants, is *fulness*. We all speak of the fulness of the gospel, implying that there are parts elsewhere which come together in this dispensation. The Lord uses the word *fulness* for other things, too. He speaks of receiving, eventually, the fulness of truth. He spoke to the Prophet Joseph from, apparently, a record of John that we have not yet received in full, but are promised we will someday, should we prove worthy. Having taught him John's testimony of Christ, how He moved from grace to grace and degree to degree, the Savior then said to Joseph: "I give unto you these sayings that you may understand and know how to worship, and know what you worship, that you may come unto the Father in my name [that's what worship is], and in due time receive of his fulness. For if you keep my commandments you shall receive of his fulness, and be glorified in me, as I am glorified in the Father; therefore, I say unto you, you shall receive grace for grace" (D&C 93:19–20). That is sacred truth, that we are in the full sense to become both recipients and outgiving servants of the Lord and that, if we are, these powers distill into our souls.

You know of the revelation the Prophet received in Liberty Jail: "Let virtue garnish thy thoughts unceasingly; then shall thy confidence wax strong in the presence of God; and the doctrine of the priesthood shall distil upon thy soul as the dews from heaven" (D&C 121:45). The fulness of truth, the fulness of the Holy Ghost, the fulness of the priesthood, and the fulness of the glory of the Father are all phrases that are current in connection with the temple and cannot be received anywhere else, nowhere else on the planet. You cannot receive the fulness that the Lord has for you without coming through the temple and having the temple come through you.

That leads us to the word for *G*, the glory of the Lord. In the worldly sense people say that somebody aspires to glory or somebody achieved glory in a given way—a calling, athletics, achievement. But we're talking about the glory of God, which, we are taught, includes intelligence—"The glory of God is intelligence" (D&C 93:36)—and then that is subdivided into light and truth. The fulness of the glory of the Father, surely, would then include those. But let me add that in the Doctrine and Covenants we're also taught something about marriage and family as the everlasting covenant (see D&C 131:2) and that the Father is a Father indeed, with you and me as begotten sons and daughters unto the Eternal Father (see D&C 76:24). Therefore we believe there is a Heavenly Mother, that priesthood and parenthood are intertwined, and that to become truly glorious is to become like them, with the powers of creation and procreation given us forever. The culminating ordinance of the house of the Lord, which we call sealing, creates eternal families.

I have recollection of a conversation with a man who had felt that in order to serve the Lord fully he must never marry. He believed in what is called celibacy, and he also believed that in the life to come there can be and will be no such possibilities, as we know here, of family relationships; they will be obliterated and we will be single and individual and saintly people forever. I said to him, before taking him for a tour of the then-undedicated Provo Temple, "Before we go, dear brother, can I get two things clear? Otherwise you won't understand what you're going to see."

I asked him, "Why don't you want to marry?"

He said, after some thought, "Well, because the things of this world do not finally matter."

I said, "Notice that you've made two assumptions. You've assumed that marriage is of this world only. Do you really know that? And secondly, you've assumed that anything that has to do with this earth is, for that very reason, to be rejected or somehow transcended."

He said, "Well, that's it, that's the truth."

I said, "Well, then, you have changed the Bible."

He said, "What do you mean?"

I said, "Blessed are the meek, for they shall inherit what?"

He said, "The earth" (see Matthew 5:5).

I said, "That's right, but in your view, who wants it?"

We have the unique insight that heaven and earth are to come together, that what many religions have split apart has been comprehensively united. For example, the physical body, which the Lord calls the temple of God (D&C 93:35), and the spirit constitute a soul (see D&C 88:15); the Lord Jesus Christ lived and died to exalt the soul, the whole of man, and wholeness ultimately means holiness. And the holiest of all achievements in this world and the next is to give your powers of creation and procreation mutually in the sacred relationship of marriage.

My friend did not change his mind, but our discussion deepened my own perception of how glorious our Father's plan is.

The glory of God is spoken of in Doctrine and Covenants 132, and the fulness of the glory of the Father is the fulness and "continuation of the seeds" (v. 19). No more literal word could be used for the power bred in us by reason of our own birth to beget posterity. Family is glory and will be extended, intensified, and increased forever. This earth will become the home of the truly sanctified, those who will follow in the way of the Father and His companion, who show us a marvelous pattern of immortality and eternal life.

I mentioned earlier the idea of rebirth. You have all been born as spirit children and, as such, have a divine nature. You have now been born of mortal parents and have been privileged, then, with a body, which is a step forward in your progression, not a step back. The body is not a prison house. It can become distorted, it can become perverted, and it can become in many ways a burden, but that is not the divine intent.

We are, instead, to proceed to watch and pray, that our bodies may be developed into the very likeness of our spirits, which are divine, and ultimately, then, become, as it were, a product of another birth, through which Jesus becomes, in the process of ordinances, our Father. It is proper to use the word *Father* for Jesus, for He says in Doctrine and Covenants 93:22: "All those who are begotten through me [through the ordinances] are partakers of the glory of the same [meaning His role as the Firstborn of the Father], and are the church of the Firstborn."

Imagine: He has sacrificed for us in order that we can inherit what He alone could claim to be, the firstborn. He is saying: "It will be as if you were; all of the blessings and powers that have been bestowed upon me are now transmitted to you if you are willing to come to me." "Those who are begotten through me are partakers of the glory of the same."

There will be another birth ahead of us, and that's called the resurrection. And then the promise that we can be like Him will be literal and complete.

Let me turn now to personal words and testimony. I could take you to the very place, when I was in graduate school in California, where I was reading in a book by Parley P. Pratt, called *The Key to the Science of Theology,* a chapter called "Laws of Marriage and Procreation." I probably marked some way, with a bookmark or turning down the leaf, a paragraph of which the following is a paraphrase: "The practice of these principles and ordinances [and he had just summarized the whole pattern] has begun to regenerate the race." And then he indicated that this is reversing the tide of degeneracy which has been in the world, beginning not so much with Adam, but with the first man named Cain, who sold, as it were, his birthright, and became not the transmitter of life, but the destroyer; he became the first murderer. The laws of degeneration have been working in the race, but the gospel of Jesus Christ will regenerate the race. And Brother Pratt described the effects of the Spirit on each individual.[2]

My wife and I were interviewed some time ago by the very man who interviewed President Hinckley, Mike Wallace. We were at the open house of the Manhattan Temple. At some point in our chat with him (by the way, he had great regard for President Hinckley), he said something like this, looking at my wife: "Why are Mormon women so lovely?" We learned later that he has not had a happy married life; he's had four wives (not simultaneously). Before Ann could answer, I thought of Parley P. Pratt, and I said, "It's the best-kept beauty secret in the world. It is the Spirit of God." Parley P. Pratt taught that the Spirit "develops beauty of person, form and features."[3]

Then Mike Wallace turned to Ann, and she said, "It's fidelity." That's a great answer. She had in mind fidelity in the sense of honoring and keeping our covenants with Christ, but also honoring our covenants with each other: fidelity in marriage. And she also meant faithfulness in marking and walking the path that Christ has laid out for us. That does make a difference, even in our physical appearance.

I testify that that is so. I believe that in the Church itself not everyone is aware of how conspicuous that beauty and that light is in the eyes and faces of the faithful, but those who have the same spirit recognize it. Jesus said: "My sheep hear my voice, and I know them, and they follow me" (John 10:27). I suggest to you that the Lord's sheep know His other sheep and recognize when He is at work in their lives and when they have the Spirit. That is a temple outcome. It comes with worshiping and honoring in the Lord's sanctuary.

It was during the same period when I had been, I think, a little skeptical, a little troubled, about the whole idea of ritual and ceremony, when I wondered if we really had to do these particular things in order to receive particular blessings, that President David

O. McKay came to a gathering in Los Angeles. He came in order to require a sacrifice of the Saints to build the temple. One of the between-the-lines messages I have for you today is that I hope you will make some sacrifices, both in inner promises and in temporal terms, and otherwise, to help temples be built in your midst, because I believe from Church history that there has never been a glorious outpouring in a temple dedication that wasn't preceded by genuine sacrifice on the part of the Saints. I ask you to contribute to temple building whenever and wherever you can.

On that occasion in Los Angeles, President McKay asked for a million dollars from the local Saints and had pledge cards before the meeting was over for that amount, and more. Then he spoke about the temple. I will mention only the details except for the core statement that I have cherished and that bent, as it were, the twig in me and has grown and grown ever since.

He said: "Brothers and sisters, I believe there are few, even temple workers, who comprehend the full meaning and power of the temple endowment. Seen for what it is, it is the step-by-step ascent into the eternal presence. If our young people could only glimpse it, it would be the most powerful spiritual motivation of their lives."

I resolved that day, because of what happened in my heart, always to raise my voice in testifying of the temple and never in criticizing it. And I resolved to carry out as best I could my dream of finding a queen who would share with me the total conviction that the temple is ours, made for us and prepared for us, and that out of that could come a family who would love the Lord Jesus Christ as nothing else in the universe. I bear testimony that, now that the years have passed, whatever is good and true and beautiful in our lives and the lives of our children is rooted in the Christ, who is a great Giver of the privileges of temples—temple building, temple worship, and temple fulfillment.

3

THE TEMPLE AND THE MYSTERIES OF GODLINESS

Come with me to a place called Kirtland, Ohio, and recall that the people asked, essentially, "Why, O why, when we hardly have enough for hominy and milk, do we have to build a temple? What is a temple? And why at such great cost?" At one point the Prophet replied, saying in essence, "The Angel Gabriel couldn't explain it to you now. But have faith and continue and the Lord will make it plain."[1] According to Elder John A. Widtsoe, the Kirtland Temple, using the measuring rod of the widow's mite—what they had in proportion to what they gave—cost more per capita than any other building in American religious history.[2] An unprecedented sacrifice! That sacrifice was met, as you all know, with an unprecedented outpouring of the Lord's Spirit.

They met in the temple and waited on the Lord by candle-light all night. I have found no record of anyone falling asleep. There was such a jubilee of feeling close to the Lord and being filled with joy that the people went from house to house to visit each other, sharing their experiences, then giving blessings to each other. One of them wrote in his journal that he thought the Millennium had come. He thought all temptation and all trial, even the desire for sin, was past.[3] The Prophet had to stand up on one occasion and say, in effect, "Brethren, this is all of God, but the opposite will come. There will be new onslaughts of trial."[4] To the Twelve he said specifically, "God will feel after you, and He will take hold of you and wrench your very heart strings, and, if you cannot stand it you will not be fit for an inheritance in the Celestial Kingdom of God."[5]

That was all too prophetic. You know the sequel. Within months there were new seeds of apostasy and bitterness: the failure of the Kirtland bank and the assigning of blame. One-half of those who were at the time faithful fell away. One-half of the Council of the Twelve—six men—apostatized. Of the remaining six, four had times of trouble and disaffection. The wrenching came. After great tribulations, our scriptures tell us, come the blessings (see D&C 58:4). On the other side of that, after great blessings come further trials. That's the nature of life. You can all testify of that from your own experience.

So after that sacrifice they were driven out. Three different times in Missouri they dedicated places for temples, but they were never able to get a shovel into the ground to start building. The Prophet Joseph made a special trip to the very center of Zion—Independence, Missouri—and dedicated land there. They dedicated Adam-ondi-Ahman for a temple. They dedicated a site in Far West. Not until Nauvoo, after having been through the crucible again, were they able to undertake the actual construction of a temple. That one took all the people's time and energies for nearly three years. How long was it actually used? Less than six weeks after its formal dedication. And it cost about a million dollars. Genuine sacrifice!

How could the Prophet have led them to make this tremendous sacrifice to be used for just six weeks? That temple was ripped as it were from its roots, destroyed by fire and then a cyclone. When they came across the plains to the alkali soil of the West (you know the story), Brigham with his cane said, "Here we will build a temple of our God."[6] Yes, it's there. It took forty years of building. Three other temples were finished before it was.

Why all this?

Some glimpses: The Prophet in one temple sermon in Nauvoo addressed a woman, a mother, who had been bereft of her son. Joseph said to her, "You shall have glad tidings today." This sister believed the scripture that talks about rebirth, that there is no access to the kingdom of God except through baptism. Her child had not been baptized. And the Prophet introduced the principle of baptism for the dead (we always say). But there are no dead. Those who are in the spirit world are very much alive. "This is your privilege: You can go into the waters of baptism for your loved ones." And, he added another phrase, "for those whom we have much friendship for."[7]

The instant reaction to that sermon was that people rushed down to the Mississippi (the temple wasn't finished, and the font wasn't finished), and began baptisms for about a hundred people. No witnesses, no records—women were baptized for men, men for women—and the Prophet literally had to run down to the river and say, "Wait, wait, we have to do this in order."[8]

It is the desire expressed here that I want to describe. Do you care about those you truly love? Do you want to bring to them the same blessings you have received? Of course.

There is much more. The Prophet taught in a sermon in

Nauvoo that "we need the temple more than we need anything else."⁹ Why?

Doctrine and Covenants 84:23–25 helps provide the answer. It tells of how Moses tried for forty years to prepare the children of Israel to go with him up to the mountain to have face-to-face communion with God. He failed. Tradition says Moses became unworthy of the Jewish people, the Israelites. Our scriptures say just the opposite. They became unworthy of him. The Lord swore in His wrath, so it says, that they should not enter into His rest while in the wilderness. Entering into His rest doesn't mean cessation of all activities. It means the rest that comes to your soul when you get out of the spiritual wilderness and are able to know and commune with the living God. Moses was taken out of their midst, says the passage, and the holy priesthood also.

Verses 20 and 21 say, "In [that higher priesthood and in] the ordinances thereof, the power of godliness is manifest [unto men and women in the flesh]. And without the ordinances thereof, and the authority of the priesthood, the power of godliness is not manifest unto men in the flesh." A categorical statement.

Whatever the powers of godliness are, they come to us in mortality through ordinances and in no other way. The highest ordinances are the ordinances of the house of God. All else is preparatory to them. Moses' people were not worthy of them. So, the Prophet taught, it was not Moses with the higher priesthood but Joshua with the lesser priesthood who crossed the Jordan and led the people into the promised land. Moses remained on Mount Nebo.

History repeats itself. The Prophet Joseph Smith yearned with his whole soul to be the modern Moses and lead at least the first company of Saints to sanctuary, to "the mountain of the Lord's house," which he had prophesied would one day be established.

He was denied that privilege, in part because his own people could not believe he was a prophet when he said, "All they want is me and my brother Hyrum, they won't touch you, they won't harm a hair of your heads."[10] They were not fully worthy of the Prophet, as the ancients were not. But the Prophet did live to confer upon the Twelve all of the higher ordinances. The temple wasn't finished, and so it was performed in the upper room of Joseph's store.[11] In a meeting that was certainly the most important summary meeting of his life, he conferred everything—keys, authorities, powers—upon them, and then commissioned Brigham Young and Wilford Woodruff to see that these truths were systematized and eventually presented as they are in the temple. He then told those twelve men that upon them now rested the charge to lead the Saints to what they needed the most and to eventually prepare the whole world, every man and every woman, for temples and the privilege of communion with the living God. Wilford Woodruff said fifty years later, "I shall never forget that."[12] They did it. You and I are the blessed recipients.

Aside from work for those we love and aside from receiving our own privileges, the temple is a place of learning and the only place for some kinds of learning that go directly to our spirits, to our core, to the very depths of our souls. "A house of learning," says Doctrine and Covenants 88. One who has written brilliantly about this is Elder John A. Widtsoe. He became the author of what was then the Temple Index Bureau, updated now with computers. He became one of the leading directors of the Genealogical Society of Utah. He became a member of the Council of the Twelve. In an article titled "Temple Worship," he wrote, "The endowment is so richly symbolic that only a fool would attempt to describe it; it is so packed full of revelations to those who exercise their strength to seek and see, that no human words can explain or make clear the possibilities that reside in the temple service. The endowment which was given by revelation can best be understood by revelation."[13]

Thus we may come to know the mysteries of godliness. *Mystery* is a word that we use negatively, usually for things that don't matter and are presently beyond our ken. Such mysteries we are counseled to avoid. In contrast, "the mysteries of godliness" are, we know from modern scholarship, the ordinances of godliness. "I advise you all," said Joseph Smith, "to go on to perfection and search deeper and deeper into the mysteries of Godliness."[14] It is a commandment. Where are we to search? In the house of God. Why there? Because the temple is dedicated to that purpose, because there we make covenants to be true to what we understand, not just learning out of curiosity but absorbing into our souls what we most need to understand. And there we covenant to keep these sacred things sacred.

Joseph Smith wrote from Liberty Jail: "The things of God are of deep import; and time, and experience, and careful and ponderous and solemn thoughts can only find them out. Thy mind, O man, if thou wilt lead a soul into salvation, must stretch as high as the utmost heavens, and search into and contemplate the darkest abyss, and the broad expanse of eternity—thou must commune with God."[15] He had time and experience and careful and ponderous and solemn thoughts in that jail, for he yearned for the same privilege within the sanctuary. He was denied it. He did not live to see the Nauvoo Temple finished. He said in a discourse given in Nauvoo: "If it should be [the] will of God that I might live to behold that temple completed, . . . I will say, Oh Lord, it is enough. Lord, let thy servant depart in peace."[16] But it didn't happen.

Parley P. Pratt spoke at the dedication of a cornerstone of the

Salt Lake Temple. He talked about communion with those who are beyond. He referred to peepings and mutterings and superstitions and Halloween kinds of activities in the world. But then, he said, there is authentic, intimate, revelatory experience with those who are tied to us by family ties and by the sacrifices they have made in their lives for us.[17] Now, perhaps according to covenant, we are here to respond by doing in the temple what we can do for them.

Asked about the spirit world, the Prophet Joseph spoke about disembodied spirits: "Enveloped in flaming fire, they are not far from us, and know . . . our thoughts, feelings, and motions and are often pained therewith."[18] And they likewise often rejoice therewith. They "are not idle spectators."[19] Somehow there are laws that enable them to have some influence upon us and we upon them. In the temple these laws are fulfilled. Parley P. Pratt taught that, for the pure in heart, when we receive communication from "kindred spirits, . . . spirit communes with spirit, thought meets thought, soul blends with soul, in all the raptures of mutual, pure, and eternal love."[20]

We do not comprehend what a blessing to them these ordinances are. In the resurrection, Joseph taught Horace Cummings, they will fall at the feet of those who have done their work, kiss their feet, embrace their knees, and manifest the most exquisite gratitude.[21]

Wilford Woodruff, who dedicated the Salt Lake Temple, taught that there will be few if any who will not receive the ordinances of the temple when they are performed for them.[22] Elder John W. Taylor, while attending the Manti Temple dedication, concluded that only one in ten would refuse the ordinances. He added, "How many who are kept in prison are not ready to come out?"[23]

What an assurance, when I go with my wife through a magnificent, two-hour experience in the temple, that we may have brought two converts into the kingdom of God. In two hours!

With Wilford Woodruff I testify that this work can be understood only by the spirit of revelation. "There was nothing made known," said Joseph Smith, speaking of the day he taught some of the Twelve the ordinances of the temple, "but what will be made known to all the Saints of the last days, so soon as they are prepared to receive." But know this, he said, they are "to be received only by the spiritual minded."[24]

The temple is also the most practical of places. Melvin J. Ballard taught that each one of us should be willing to take to the temple our worst problems, and he was talking about hard, down-to-earth, even physical problems. You pray, you fast. But if you don't get your answer, he said, I'll tell you what to do: go to the house of the Lord, and in the silence of those precincts, as you are serving others, the Lord will bless you.[25] We've mentioned the experience of John A. Widtsoe. As a soil chemist, he struggled to draw a mountain of data together and make it applicable. It did not work. He finally called his wife. "Let's go to the temple and forget the failure." In the temple his answer came. That resulted in two books and in a revolution in agrarian practice. I know people who have had the most wrenching soul trials, such as that in my own life when my brother went down in a plane crash. I know for myself and for others that the place of the most tangible comfort is the house of the Lord.

When Joseph Smith and Oliver Cowdery were at the pulpit at the east end of the Kirtland Temple, they heard from the Lord Himself these words: "Behold, I have accepted this house, and my name shall be here; and I will manifest myself to my people in mercy in this house. . . . And this is the beginning of the blessing which shall be poured out upon the heads of my people" (D&C 110:7, 10).

Notice: "my name shall be here." Solomon pled for that when he dedicated the ancient temple (see 1 Kings 8:28–29). What does it mean? There are depths beyond depths of meaning. You are required as disciples of Christ to come once in seven days and covenant anew to take upon you the name of Jesus Christ. In the house of the Lord you come to take upon you His name in the fullest sense. Why all the emphasis on fulness? Well, there is a promise that we will one day have a fulness of truth. That is temple-related. We are promised the fulness of the Holy Ghost. Joseph Smith prayed for that at the Kirtland Temple dedication (see D&C 109:15). And we are promised within the temple the fulness of the priesthood.

Likewise, we are promised that in the temple the Lord's name will be put upon us. It means at its root that we become His. The answer to "Who am I?" can never be complete unless it answers "Whose am I?" You are the son or daughter of a King—the Father Himself. Through the ordinances you are begotten spiritually through His Son. You become heir to His throne. That is a worldly way of saying it. But it is true. An old Jewish proverb says that the worst thing the evil inclination can ever do to you is to make you forget that you are the son or daughter of a king. I don't know how you can forget that in the temple. You take His name.

To receive Him fully is to receive the fulness of His Atonement. Think about it—the fulness of the at-one-ment that Jesus Christ wrought by the shedding of His own blood. The Atonement was, and is, to enable us to overcome, through His grace and healing power, three things: ignorance, sin, and death. Hence I often say that the temple is a matter of life and death.

"It is impossible for a man to be saved in ignorance" (D&C

131:6). This passage refers to a specific kind of ignorance. The preceding verse is talking about sealing, about coming to know by revelation through the power of the holy priesthood not only that Jesus is the Christ, but also that a relationship has been forged between you and Jesus Christ. It is a testimony that there is light at the end of the tunnel, that He is making you His. How do you come to know that? I can tell you that the promise does pertain to the temple. And we may come to a like testimony about temple sealings to our progenitors and our children.

The Savior said that He came that men "might have life, and that they might have it more abundantly" (John 10:10). Life, abundant life, is pluralized in the teachings of Joseph Smith as "eternal lives" (D&C 132:24).

You are all alive in several ways and to certain degrees. You are alive intellectually: you think, you study, you teach. There is, no matter what else we do each day, the life of the mind.

Then there is the life of the heart. The word in Hebrew is *leb*, "heart," the inmost throbbing center. A hard heart is different from a malleable, tender heart. Christ's heart is tender. Those who come to Him feeling mercy and gratitude for His mercy are tenderized in the very center of their being.

We seek life in another way. It is the creative life. It is lodged in the cry of ancient Israelite fathers and mothers: "Give me children, or else I die" (Genesis 30:1). This is the life of creation and procreation.

I testify that in the house of the Lord all three of these modes of life are enhanced and magnified and increased. Therein we are promised that whatever our age or the decline and disabilities that we experience here, we will one day enter in at the gate to eternal lives. On that day of renewal, we will emerge into a celestial condition, into the "fulness of the glory of the Father" (D&C 93:16).

There the glorious privilege of priesthood, parenthood, and god-hood come together as one. There, forever, will be the reunion of the separated. As this is the crowning ordinance of the house of God, it is also the crowning truth of the gospel.

President Brigham Young was once approached by two sisters, each of whom wanted a divorce. I paraphrase his response: "If you could only see your husband as he will be in the glorious resurrection, this very husband you now say you despise, your first impulse would be to kneel and worship him."[26] He said the same thing to husbands who had "fallen out of love" with their wives. Those are mighty words.

That leads me to the main and final point. I haven't yet used the expression "fulness of love." Consider this passage in D&C section 88: "For intelligence cleaveth unto intelligence; wisdom receiveth wisdom; truth embraceth truth; virtue loveth virtue; light cleaveth unto light; mercy hath compassion on mercy and claimeth her own; justice continueth its course and claimeth its own; judgment goeth before the face of him who sitteth upon the throne and governeth and executeth all things" (v. 40).

In the same way, only the virtuous know true love.

In religious tradition much is said and even canonized about how God is "absolutely other." They say that not one sentence you can utter about human beings applies in any way whatever to God; God must be absolutely different, say they, or we could not love and worship Him. Joseph Smith died to get back in the world the truth that we are in fact in the image of God. In fact, that means that as a statue exactly resembles the person it represents, so man exactly resembles the nature of the Father and the Son. That's the great and glorious secret. Man and woman are theo-morphic; they are in the form of God. That is the foundation of divine-human love.

In some patterns of worship, it is thought that the way to convey our proper relationship to God is to cultivate darkness, magnify distance, use only the kinds of music, or words, or ceremonial procedures that invoke awe and even irrational fear. The testimony of the restored temple is that God the Father and His Son Jesus Christ yearn not to widen that gap but to close it. In the house of the Lord we may come to Him in light, in closeness, and in holy embrace. He promises in latter-day revelation: "I will manifest myself to my people in mercy in this house" (D&C 110:7). That is love.

I testify, speaking as one who had to be converted to this, that the temple is many things: a house of faith, a house of study, a house of learning, a house of order, a house of prayer, a house of fasting, a house of glory. But, surrounding all of those, it is a house of love. None of us receives enough love in this world, none of us. We're all in a measure love-starved and love-anxious. The Father and the Son call us to come in the spirit of sacrifice and be surrounded by that holy environment which embraces us in love.

Remember that Jesus looked out over the holy city and lamented, "O Jerusalem, Jerusalem, . . . how often would I have gathered [you] together, even as a hen gathereth her chickens under her wings, and ye would not!" (Matthew 23:37). He repeated those words to the Nephites, using three tenses: I *have* gathered you, I *would have* gathered you (speaking of those who were wiped away in a terrible earthquake), and I *will* gather you (see 3 Nephi 10:4–6).

I suggest to you that here is another symbolic allusion to the temple. The wings of a mother hen are intimate, and protective, and warm. In 3 Nephi the Savior added another phrase about the hen and her wandering chicks: "I . . . have nourished you" (10:4). The Jews speak of the temple as the navel, the *emphallos,* of the earth, the very place that heaven brings nutriment to earth. Jesus wept because He had been unable to gather his people. Modern revelation tells us He wanted to gather them in order to bring them into His sanctuary to reveal to them and pour out upon them the glories of His temple.[27] But they would not. They hated their own blood. Our generation is slipping more and more into the same mud.

I have stood on the Mount of Olives. There came down on me a prophetic and anticipatory sense that a day will come when He will descend in like manner as He once ascended from that very mount. Angels heralded His birth into the world. So I speculate that a choir welcomed Him home. We have been promised that some of us may be present to welcome Him as he descends. We will sing a new song. He has already given us the words (D&C 88:99–102). Inspired knowledge and maybe even memory will enable us to sing to His glory on that occasion. The very touch of His foot, His glorified and celestial foot, will change the world and eventually the whole human family. A temple will be in place in Jerusalem by then, perhaps more than one. There and elsewhere, worthy people will recognize Him and glory in His presence. This time there will be no tears except tears of joy.

I testify that this is true. I testify that temples have been built by the sacrifice of our friends and loved ones to enable us to reach them as well as the deepest part of ourselves. Beyond that I testify that in the house of the Lord, He, the Lord Himself, will manifest Himself in mercy and in love and give us the fulness of those blessings we all earnestly yearn for.

4

BLESSINGS OF THE TEMPLE

I introduce this chapter with a comment that came to me second-hand from the late President J. Reuben Clark. After going through the Harvard mania and earning my degree, I was in a position, through a strange set of circumstances, to earn a second PhD by investing only one more year. (I had already been at it for four.) I raised the issue with Elder Harold B. Lee during a stake conference. I asked for a nudge in the right direction. He said, "President Clark just returned from being released as a director of Union Pacific Railroad. He chatted with me on the way west. He said to me: 'Now that I am eighty-plus years old, all of the distinctions that I have achieved, all else that deals with getting through life, has paled alongside only one real question: How have I lived in relation to the gospel, and what about my family?'" Then Brother Lee said to me: "Spend more time with your family! Life is for living!" That was good counsel to me at the time.

Where does one find a balance staff? The balance staff is the temple.

This brief chapter will be based on some insights gained through living and breathing and feeling the Jewish tradition about the centrality of the temple. The Midrash says things were missing from the second temple that were present in the first.[1] First was the sacred fire. In Solomon's temple and at its dedication, there was an outpouring they call the *Shechinah*, the glory of God, like fire. That did not happen at the second temple. In the first temple they had the gift of prophecy, but not in the second. In the first temple they had a holy anointing, but not in the second temple. The first temple had the Urim and Thummim, an instrument for somehow discerning the will of God. That was not in the second temple. Finally, they had the Ark of the Covenant in the first temple. The Ark was most significant because it contained the tables of the law given to Moses.

The very weight and power of the Spirit (such that we cannot deny) is there in the temple. It is there, waiting for us. We are invited to come to this sacred sanctuary in the spirit of dedication, for more. At the dedication of the Kirtland Temple, all of those things missing from the second Jewish temple were present. (This preparatory temple made way for the eventual complete temple experience, of which the most magnificent example is in Salt Lake City.) There was an outpouring of Spirit so real it was like fire. Neighbors, not of the faith, came running, thinking it was fire. Father Joseph Smith stood up and asked, "Is the building on fire?" His son Joseph said, "No, Father, our prayer has been answered. We asked that it would be as on the days of Pentecost, as encircling tongues of fire. It has happened."[2] In the Kirtland Temple there was a Urim and Thummim in an upstairs room. In that temple all experienced the gift of prophecy, an unprecedented outpouring of it in the Church up to that point. It was rich and powerful. There was a holy anointing under divine direction. Upstairs in Joseph's translation room were books—being translated from Moses and Abraham—and other sacred scripture that had not been made known to the world for generations. And there was a prophet of God. It's incredible that we should have inherited in this generation what was so long lost. But that is only the beginning.

When as a mere nineteen-year-old missionary I had the privilege of receiving the blessings of the temple, one thing was clear to me. Within that set of walls, I felt something almost as tangible as light and the warmth and peace of a warm blanket, heavier than air. I felt it. I didn't want to leave it. I now think I understand the line in the Prophet's Kirtland prayer that all who enter might be "constrained to acknowledge . . . that it is [his] house, a place of [his] holiness" (D&C 109:13). We don't believe in compulsion in this Church. What does constraint mean? It means that we feel the very weight and power of the Spirit so strongly that we cannot deny is there. It is there, waiting for us. We are invited to come to this sacred sanctuary, in the spirit of dedication, for more.

Hugh Nibley, in his book on the Egyptian papyri, taught of the Egyptian temple. Although he saw all kinds of parallels with the restored temple, he finally summarized by saying the temple is a powerhouse. It is both filled with power and is a generator of power.[3] Endowment means, among other things, being surrounded and then permeated with the power of God: "endowed with power from on high" (D&C 105:11). That is what we are called to go back and back again for. We can then concentrate, receive, and carry this power into our own mini-temples, which are our homes.

Ann and I had a temple courtship. We were idealistic; the

temple was to us the symbol of everything glorious in marriage and promise. We can now rejoice that our family, our children, have taken hold of this. In successive home evenings, we prepared our children for the Provo Temple dedication. Although the children were small, they could understand about a sanctuary, a sacred place, a house of prayer, a place where all dress in beautiful, symbolic white, and so on. We went to the dedication fasting. Some of you may remember the gathering in the Marriott Center with the huge screen. All of our family, even the youngest, felt and gained a temple testimony. God's power is there.

The Jews now go not to the remnant of the temple, or even of the foundation of the temple, or even of the platform on which the temple stood (all are destroyed), but to a remnant of the retaining wall that provided the stonework, or buttress, for the superstructure. Annually, on *Tishbe-av* (the ninth of the month of Av), they weep and cry out in mourning for the loss of their temple. The most orthodox have faith that there will be a new one. The temple is the culminating place of kinship and love. As if it were a magnifying glass that catches the light of the sun (*S-o-n* as well as *s-u-n*), the temple somehow enables us to see and feel and be filled with divine love.

We often talk about the family unit as one set of parents and children. This is a recent twentieth-century idea. Family in earlier centuries meant at least four generations. Family is the whole family. We speak of doing work for the dead when, in fact, we only work for the living, including those living in the spirit world. The power that comes from the assurance of that kinship and the sense that we are serving unselfishly creates a return wave of love that is real. Guidance, protection, loving influence—all these the house of God makes possible for us.

Now a word of testimony. While we were in the Jerusalem

Center, the numbers of visitors increased. First the curious came, and then many others followed, wanting to see. How many? A hundred thousand in one year. We encouraged them to write, in a guest book, their impressions. Is the Jerusalem Center a temple? No, it isn't. It is a house of learning; but it feels like a temple. We have Jewish friends who have used that exact language. Often those who write say, in Hebrew or sometimes in Arabic, "I feel shalom" or "salaam." What is that? *Peace.* We heard a little child say, pulling on her mother's skirts, "Imma, Imma [that means mother], can we live here?" Why? Because of the spirit of peace she felt there.

President Howard W. Hunter gave a dedicatory prayer for the Jerusalem Center. We were privileged to hear it. He asked that everyone who entered, whether to learn or to teach or for any other purpose, would feel the Spirit of the Lord. That blessing is tangibly fulfilled. Perhaps the world would not understand the difference such a dedication has made to that glorious structure. God's power now resides in that building, and we had the privilege day after day of basking in a tangible peace. I testify that this is even more true of our sacred sanctuaries, the temples of the Lord. The temple is a template to help us find and recover our bearings.

Twice a month Ann and I go to the temple. We gain something each time. I hear people say: "But it's the same thing. How can you stand sheer repetition?" For the same reason that Hugh Nibley and his wife did. I used to watch him. He concentrated; he focused. It is never just "the same thing." This week there is greater depth of understanding; this week there is more of putting things together. In the temple Hugh Nibley was like a child on Christmas morning. So can we be.

I pray that in the moments of anguish and stress and burden

that will come to all of us, we will recognize that God has given us a balance staff, which, as the Prophet Joseph once said, "holds the storm."[4] That is the temple. It is the Lord's house. He is there through His Spirit, and He has promised to manifest Himself in mercy unto His children throughout their lives.

5

HOUSE OF GLORY, HOUSE OF LIGHT, HOUSE OF LOVE

Truman G. Madsen and Ann N. Madsen

TRUMAN: Like you, we are keenly aware that the subject of the temple is both intimate and sacred. In 1893, shortly before the dedication of the Salt Lake Temple, Elder Franklin D. Richards said: "The temples are full of telegrams from the heavenly world for you. . . . The blessings of heaven are treasured up there, and these temples are the great repositories of eternal life, glory, honor and immortality, waiting for the children of God to come up and bring their offerings of broken hearts and contrite spirits, and draw upon those treasures."[1]

ANN: When Elder Richards wrote that in 1893, there were three operating temples in the world. Today there are more than 120 operating temples, with others under construction or announced. This seems to be just the beginning. Our access to temples will dramatically increase with these many new temples. In this amazing multiplication, temple dedications will no longer be rare. They may still be once in a lifetime, but now that glorious experience will happen to Latter-day Saints all over the world.

How can we prepare ourselves for the wonderful experience of temple worship? Let me answer that question by describing how my love for the temple began and how Truman helped me prepare for my first visit to the house of the Lord. He gave me a copy of the Doctrine and Covenants to study two hundred underlined verses that referred to the temple. There were hours of tutoring in front of the University of Utah institute building between classes. And there was a fireside series on temples at the old Eighteenth Ward in Salt Lake City, where two of the lectures were given by a young Truman G. Madsen.

Did I have a hunger for the treasures of the temple? Oh, yes! And was it satisfied? With a feast!

TRUMAN: In the final lecture of that fireside series, entitled "Personally Vital Temple Purposes," I was astonished to hear myself say in public, "In the temple I was inspired to go to Ann Nicholls and ask her to marry me." That was news to everyone—including Ann. It was even news to me. I gasped. She gasped. We have since said to our children that we had a temple courtship as well as a temple marriage.

ANN: On a beautiful June day in 1953 Truman led me to an altar in the Salt Lake Temple so that we could kneel across from each other and look into each other's eyes and into the clear blue eyes of President David O. McKay as he officiated at the ceremony that would bind us to one another from that day to this moment and then forever, according to our faithfulness.

TRUMAN: Our long experience in temple worship together began on that day fifty-five years ago. We'd like to share with you some of what we have learned in that time.

As a framework, we'll consider the following questions:

How does the temple help us see ourselves as we really are?

How does the temple help us better understand the role of women in the plan of salvation?

How do we find Christ in the temple, and how do we approach Him there?

What level of purity is necessary before we enter the temple, and how will the temple further purify us?

How do we access and understand the light and truth that is in the temple?

What can we learn in the temple about praying?

How does our love for our families and those we serve expand through temple worship?

How do we take the temple home with us, and how can the teachings of the temple transform our homes?

HOW DOES THE TEMPLE HELP US
SEE OURSELVES AS WE REALLY ARE?

ANN: In the temple we are taught the beauty of holiness, the grandeur of virtuous lives. We sometimes live far beneath our spiritual potential,[2] and when we fall short, Satan reminds us of our inadequacies and seeks to pull us down to even lower levels. Yet "daily a voice [in each of us] demands that we ascend, that we rise . . . to the peak of the mountain."[3] Isaiah invites us powerfully, "Come ye, and let us go up to the mountain of the Lord, to the house of the God of Jacob; and he will teach us of his ways, and we will walk in his paths. . . . Come ye, and let us walk in the light of the Lord" (Isaiah 2:3–5).

TRUMAN: Jesus the Christ spoke of Himself as a temple. Likewise the apostle Paul chooses that highest of names for us: "Know ye not that ye are the temple of God, and that the Spirit of

God dwelleth in you?" (1 Corinthians 3:16). And the Lord said, "The elements are the tabernacle of God; yea, man is the tabernacle of God, even temples" (D&C 93:35). That is the vision He offers us of the radiant beings we can become.

Everything that we can say of Christ He promises us in potential. In His dedicated temples the power of His life and Atonement and Spirit enters our lives, and His endowment of power gradually transforms us into His likeness. Two powerful words, "as if," are part of our temple experience. It is "as if" Christ Himself personally ministers and administers every promise and every covenant to us.

ANN: We *can* learn to be like Christ. He has "called us to glory and virtue," as Peter explained, and has "given unto us exceeding great and precious promises: that by these [we] might be partakers of the divine nature" (2 Peter 1:3–4). His temple ordinances act as a compass to point the way. It is not a crooked path. It is straight and narrow, and it requires our hearts, total commitment, and faith.

Elder Henry B. Eyring says it so well: "It is uncomplicated. We simply submit to the authority of the Savior and promise to be obedient to whatever He commands."[4]

When Thomas asked Jesus, "How can we know the way [or the path]?" He replied simply, "I am the way" (John 14:5–6).

TRUMAN: The temple helps us see ourselves as we really are, divine children of our Heavenly Father with the potential to become like Him. It teaches us that this is how God sees us.

Two little girls were sitting together in Sunday School. One whispered to the other, "My grandfather is the prophet." After thinking that over, the other replied, "My grandfather is God."

In the eyes of our heavenly parents we are noble children, children of destiny. Just as we see great promise and good in our children and perfection in our grandchildren, He says to you, "You're wonderful just as you are! You're beautiful now! You can become a queen!"

ANN: One afternoon in the New England Mission home, Truman invited me to join him at the close of a missionary zone leaders' meeting. He found me upstairs in our room, exhausted.

As Truman left, I sank to my knees and said simply, "If you have something you want me to say, Lord, just tell me and I'll say it. But I'm running on empty." I had learned such prayers are answered. I started to go down, and I remember right where I was on the stairs when I had an unmistakable impression: "Tell them they are my sons." And in a flash I knew as never before what it means that I am His daughter. The power of that experience still resonates in me.

TRUMAN: As spirits, we are born of heavenly parentage. In the quickening processes of the temple we become Christ's—in mind, spirit, and body. Thus, when Joseph Smith first sent the Twelve to England he instructed them to teach: "Being born again, comes by the Spirit of God through ordinances."[5]

The highest ordinances of rebirth are given to us in the temple. Jesus submitted to all these ordinances, received the powers of godliness, and after the Mount of Transfiguration said, "All power is given unto me both in heaven and in earth" (Matthew 28:18). He said to His disciples at the climax of His life, "Be of good cheer; I have overcome the world" (John 16:33).

If we submit in that same pattern, we, through Him, can overcome the world. How is it done? Modern revelation tells us. "For whoso is faithful unto the obtaining these two priesthoods of which I have spoken, and the magnifying their calling, are sanctified by the Spirit unto the renewing of their bodies" (D&C 84:33).

Joseph Smith taught that through this process we become a new creation by the Holy Ghost and that the fulness of the Holy Ghost is given in the temple (see D&C 109:15). We are purged of sin and sinfulness and we are prepared for His presence. We are enlightened by His Spirit. And we are transformed by it. He even taught that this process has, as he put it, a "visible effect."[6]

I have seen beautiful, white-haired sisters in the temple and have thought to myself, *Who can believe that there is anything but exalting truth in our temples when they see a face like yours?* Their faces are the mirror of consecrated lives. My grandfather once remarked that a photo gallery of such women would convert the world to Christ.

HOW DOES THE TEMPLE HELP US BETTER UNDERSTAND THE ROLE OF WOMEN IN THE PLAN OF SALVATION?

TRUMAN: Hugh Nibley studied world ritual for more than fifty years. One of his illuminating articles on the temple appears in the *Encyclopedia of Mormonism*. He speaks of the temple as "Eve's show." This insight not only is emblazoned in the temple ordinances from first to last but is presupposed by them.

Our understanding of Eve is a radical inversion of many other religious traditions. The Pearl of Great Price describes God breathing into Adam the breath of life, or *ruach* in Hebrew. Joseph Smith taught, however, that when *ruach* is applied to Eve, it should be translated as "the breath of lives."[7]

Patricia Holland added an important insight about the nature of Eve's motherhood: "Could we consider this one possibility about our eternal female identity . . . ? Eve was given the identity of 'the mother of all living' years, decades, perhaps centuries before she ever bore a child. It would appear that her motherhood preceded her maternity, just as surely as the perfection of the Garden preceded the struggles of mortality. I believe *mother* is one of those very carefully chosen words, one of those rich words, with meaning after meaning after meaning. We must not, at all costs, let that word divide us. I believe with all my heart that it is first and foremost a statement about our nature, not a head count of our children."[8]

So Eve is a magnificent mother, but she is more. She is the life of those around her, her husband most of all. She feeds him, clothes him, loves him. But men are alive in at least three ways other than physically: intellectually, spiritually, and creatively. Woman innately has power to enliven, quicken, nourish, and magnify all these lives. In the temple we learn from Eve many essential roles of womanhood.

Some will argue, Was not Eve the terrible cause of the fall of the human race? Is she not justly maligned? Is not woman intrinsically evil?

On the contrary. The temple teaches there is something intrinsically good, even divine, in woman. She is the heroine who led the way into this obstacle course of mortality. Eve and then Adam would partake of the fruit, with drastic, yet ultimately glorifying, consequences. In the book of Moses, Eve sees unerringly and comforts Adam: "Were it not for our transgression we never should have had seed, and never should have known good and evil, and the joy of our redemption" (Moses 5:11). Eve in truth is inspired. What could be more Christlike than her sacrificial decision to seek the redemption of our Father's family rather than avoid the bitter cup? A woman was the first to taste death and the first to witness resurrected life. That is no coincidence. It is a lasting testimony of God's trust in woman.

Hence the temple doctrine is unequivocal. Eve both receives

and gives. She is an equal partner. She did not leave the garden for trivial, selfish gratification but to open the way for the birth and rebirth of the whole human family.

A woman's blessings in the temple are transcendent.

The ultimate relationship for a man and a woman can be found in temple marriage. Many traditions tend toward a negative view of marriage as an embarrassment, a necessary evil. But in a temple perspective, God commands the grandeur, the celebration, and the perpetuation of marriage and family. Women and men are equal partners: a king only with a queen, a priest only with a priestess, a patriarch only with a matriarch. This is the eternal truth: God glories in the sanctity and beauty of woman.

If only you could have this wave of divine recognition and approval and trust fill you to the brim! It is one of the treasures of the temple. The more you look for it there, the more you will find it.

HOW DO WE FIND CHRIST IN THE TEMPLE, AND HOW DO WE APPROACH HIM THERE?

ANN: Anciently the children of Israel, led by Moses, built a sanctuary. We often refer to it as a "tabernacle," but in Hebrew it is called *ohel moade,* or the "tent of meeting"; it was the place where Moses met the Lord and spoke with Him "face to face." Our temples are also places where we can come into His presence.

In the Doctrine and Covenants we read, "My glory shall rest upon it; . . . my presence shall be there, for I will come into it, and all the pure in heart that shall come into it shall see God" (D&C 97:15–16).

TRUMAN: Elder John A. Widtsoe taught that it is a glorious promise that those who enter the temple shall see the face of God. But, he wrote, what that means to most of us for now is that "the pure in heart who go into the temples, may, there, by the Spirit of God, always have a wonderfully rich communion with God."[9]

How do we prepare ourselves to one day enter God's presence? One essential way is attending the temple. Modern revelation teaches: "Therefore, sanctify yourselves that your minds become single to God, and the days will come that you shall see him; for he will unveil his face unto you, and it shall be in his own time, and in his own way, and according to his own will" (D&C 88:68).

ANN: We are to come to the temple in reverence, open-souled, able to cultivate silence. President James E. Faust taught us at the general Young Women's meeting in 1998: "Hold your soul very still, and listen to the whisperings of the Holy Spirit. Follow the noble, intuitive feelings planted deep within your souls by Deity in the previous world. In this way you will be responding to the Holy Spirit of God and will be sanctified by truth."[10]

We are asked to be quiet and speak only in whispers in the temple. It is easy to sense why. It is so that we can learn to be comfortable communing. It is to help us find Christ in the temple.

Some years ago I wrote these lines:

> *Would God have us know silence?*
> *In this time of brazen bells*
> *Does He invite us*
> *To a place apart*
> *To bend in some secluded spot*
> *To listen?*
> *Is snow descending*
> *Soundlessly*
> *His lesson?*
> *When He calls to us*
> *In the still, small voice*
> *Elijah heard,*

Will we not have to wait,
With Elijah,
For surcease
From the wind, fire and quake
Of our daily din
That our Lord's
Own mild, yet piercing voice
Might shimmer
In our souls?
God
Whispers into enraptured silence,
"Be still
And know that I am God."

TRUMAN: We must all learn when to speak and when to keep silent. Once when I gave Ann a blessing, these words came to me: "You will know when to speak and when to keep silent." We are counseled, "Remember that that which cometh from above is sacred, and must be spoken with care, and by constraint of the Spirit . . . ; wherefore, without this there remaineth condemnation" (D&C 63:64).

We must show the Lord how far He can trust us. He surrounds our temple covenants with sobering requirements that we keep in our hearts that which is sacred.

WHAT LEVEL OF PURITY IS NECESSARY BEFORE WE ENTER THE TEMPLE, AND HOW WILL THE TEMPLE FURTHER PURIFY US?

ANN: When you think of purity, you might think of a newborn baby. Can we as adults somehow learn to approach the purity of a child? We must strive for purity of heart, purity of mind, purity of language, and purity of behavior. How can we attain conscious innocence?

The Lord has said: "Prepare yourselves, and sanctify your-selves; yea, purify your hearts, and cleanse your hands and your feet before me, that I may make you clean; that I may testify unto your Father, and your God, and my God, that you are clean from the blood of this wicked generation" (D&C 88:74–75).

We need to know what clean feels like in order to get our bearings in this sometimes muddy world. We dress in white in the temple to represent purity. We offer broken hearts and contrite spirits, as pure as we can be, and that is acceptable to a loving Father.

Isaiah says it so well: "Wash you, make you clean; put away the evil of your doings from before mine eyes; cease to do evil; . . . relieve the oppressed, . . . plead for the widow. Come now, and let us reason together, saith the Lord [Jehovah]: though your sins be as scarlet, they shall be as white as snow" (Isaiah 1:16–18). That is pure.

TRUMAN: Our weekly opportunity to cleanse ourselves is at the sacrament table. How does the sacrament help us in the puri-fying process? It reminds us regularly of our commitment to be cleansed by Jesus' blood, shed for us in the Atonement. We all know that blood stains, but the blood of Christ purges us and purifies us.

After the birth of our daughter Mindy's third child, her doctor said to me, "Your daughter is hemorrhaging. We can't stop the bleeding. A hysterectomy could save her, but she might not sur-vive that surgery."

"What are you telling me?" I asked. "I'm telling you to pray," he answered. We prayed and administered to her. Mindy, fright-ened, anxious, and weak, was trying to calm herself. She began whispering the sacrament prayers. As she lay there bleeding, she reached the phrase, "that they may do it in remembrance of the blood of thy Son, which was shed for them" (D&C 20:79). Revelations come in hospitals. Mindy was given a new understanding of the life-giving power of Christ's atoning sacrifice. She was healed, and she returned to the sacrament and the temple with added insight and gratitude.

ANN: By partaking of the symbols of Christ's body and blood, when attended by the Spirit, we are washed clean, rinsed from the grime and filth of the world in completion of the changing process we call repentance. We give away all our sins that we may know the Lord. The tiny cup of water offered us in the sacrament is enough to gradually cleanse the "inner vessel"—that part of us that only the Lord sees.

TRUMAN: As Joseph Smith and Oliver Cowdery bowed their heads in the Kirtland Temple they heard the sweetest words of acceptance we can pray to hear: "Behold, your sins are forgiven you; you are clean before me; therefore, lift up your heads and rejoice" (D&C 110:5).

Throughout our lives we can continue the refreshing and regenerating process of becoming pure. We're promised that the time can come when we will have "lost every desire for sin"[11] and will even "look upon sin . . . with abhorrence" (Alma 13:12; 27:28).

ANN: "What are these which are arrayed in white robes?" we are asked in the book of Revelation (7:13). We think of those made pure through temple worship.

President Boyd K. Packer has written, "Our labors in the temple cover us with a shield and a protection, both individually and as a people."[12]

President Carlos E. Asay of the Salt Lake Temple wrote in an

Ensign article: "I like to think of the garment as the Lord's way of letting us take part of the temple with us when we leave. It is true that we carry from the Lord's house inspired teachings and sacred covenants written in our minds and hearts. However, the one tangible remembrance we carry with us back into the world is the garment. And though we cannot always be in the temple, a part of it can always be with us to bless our lives."[13]

From the pristine white clothing worn inside the temple we take this precious part to be with us night and day. It is a daily reminder of what we have seen, heard, and felt. It shields us from the fallout of evil in the world. It helps maintain the radiance we have glimpsed in the house of the Lord.

HOW DO WE ACCESS AND UNDERSTAND THE LIGHT AND TRUTH THAT IS IN THE TEMPLE?

TRUMAN: The temple is called by the Lord "a house of *learning*," in which we will be "perfected in [our] *understanding*" (D&C 88:119; 97:14; emphasis added).

Elder John A. Widtsoe testified: "The endowment is . . . so packed full of revelations to those who exercise their strength to seek and see, that no human words can explain or make clear the possibilities that reside in the temple service. The endowment which was given by revelation can best be understood by revelation; and to those who seek most vigorously, with pure hearts, will the revelation be greatest."[14]

It is common knowledge that keeping the Word of Wisdom is a prerequisite for entering the temple. Our emphasis on the health benefits, the "run and not be weary" promise at the end of the revelation, sometimes obscures a related promise: "And shall find wisdom and great treasures of knowledge, even hidden treasures" (D&C 89:19).

Joseph Fielding Smith, as president of the Salt Lake Temple, often spoke of his favorite scripture: "That which is of God is light; and he that receiveth light, and continueth in God, receiveth more light; and that light groweth brighter and brighter until the perfect day" (D&C 50:24).

One night Elder Harold B. Lee sat with the president of the Manti Temple looking up toward the floodlighted spires. A dark storm raged around them. The temple president said, "You know, Brother Lee, that temple is never more beautiful than during a storm."[15]

Jesus said that He is the "light that shineth in darkness and the darkness comprehendeth it not" (D&C 45:7; see John 1:5). In the Greek version of John 1:5, this reads "the darkness did not overtake the light." In other words, no engulfing darkness can totally obliterate the divine light that is deep inside us. And in His temple our light cleaves unto His light, our truth embraces His truth, and our virtue loves His virtue (see D&C 88:40).

Anticipating the first temple in our dispensation, the Lord said: "If thou shalt ask, thou shalt receive revelation upon revelation, knowledge upon knowledge, that thou mayest know the mysteries and peaceable things—that which bringeth joy, that which bringeth life eternal" (D&C 42:61).

The mysteries of godliness are locked in the ordinances of godliness.

ANN: Robert L. Millet helps us understand one way we access and understand the truths that are presented to us in the temple. He has written, "We do not see things as *they* really are; we see things as *we* really are."[16]

Taking our covenants seriously transforms *us*. I heard anthropologist Professor Merlin Myers explain this once. Simply put, he said, "Scientists use mathematical symbols, a symbol system to let themselves into reality [truth]."[17] But the most powerful symbols transcend mathematics.

1. Ordinances are a symbol system (baptism, sacrament, temple ordinances, etc.).
2. Ordinances contain patterns of action or modes of behavior.
3. We act and are conditioned, and only then do we see into reality or truth.
4. Then a transformation occurs in us so we can see as God sees.

That means finally that the "temple goes through us" after many times of our "going through the temple."

Our five-year-old grandson was taught in a recent Primary sharing time that each of us has two bodies and that they are alike. Later, as he left the house to go to church, he said excitedly, "Mom, I'm going to feed my spiritual body!" That sums it up.

The temple is the Lord's university. For entrance you do not need to have a 3.8 grade-point average. To qualify, the Lord asks only that you bring a broken heart and a contrite spirit to His altar. You must be willing to consecrate yourself, with the integrity to keep sacred things in your heart and with a tremendous desire to serve the Lord Jesus Christ.

"Therefore," says the Doctrine and Covenants, "in the ordinances thereof, the power of godliness is manifest. And without the ordinances thereof, and the authority of the priesthood, the power of godliness is not manifest unto men in the flesh; for without this no man can see the face of God, even the Father, and live" (D&C 84:20–22).

Sister Wendy L. Watson taught us a related truth at a BYU devotional: "When you interact with someone repeatedly over time, it changes you. That's why what you watch on TV or read or see in magazines is so critical. So watch what you watch. Be careful with whom or what you are interacting. These recurrent interactions change your cells. They change your soul. They change your countenance."

She continued with a question: "So, who would you most want to be like? Whose image would you like engraven on your countenance? . . . The Savior entreats us to come unto Him. . . . He wants us to have increasingly repeated interactions with Him, and to really get to know Him. And because He never changes, the changes that would occur through our interaction with the Savior would all be in us. . . . As we really come unto Him, we can become like Him."

She went on to say that the Savior is the ultimate and only true and living agent for change. He is the source of all change for good. "His desire is for you to change, to have a change of heart, a change of nature. . . . In fact, He did all that He did so that you could change."[18]

Thus we are taught that "through the power and manifestation of the Spirit, while in the flesh, [we] may be able to bear his presence in the world of glory" (D&C 76:118).

Isaiah asks us who can dwell with God in everlasting burnings and answers the question powerfully: "He that walketh righteously, and speaketh uprightly; . . . that shaketh his hands from holding of bribes, that stoppeth his ears from hearing of blood, and shutteth his eyes from seeing evil; he shall dwell on high" (Isaiah 33:15–16).

I love Truman's account of his first encounter with this brightness in the temple. I cannot tell it as well as he, but I can feel it.

TRUMAN: I was sitting alone in the celestial room of the Salt Lake Temple after receiving my own endowment. I had only begun to grasp the meaning of the experience, but gradually I felt a burning of light and peace—more penetratingly than ever in my life. I felt as if I hardly wanted to breathe or move, and I sat there like a statue lest I somehow break or diminish the flow of brightness.

ANN: I had a similar feeling at the dedication of the Washington D.C. Temple in November 1974 when President Spencer W. Kimball prophesied there would be thousands of temples. I wanted to linger in the room at the close of the dedicatory services, a room so full of light. It was almost impossible to go away from the glory I felt.

WHAT CAN WE LEARN IN THE TEMPLE ABOUT PRAYING?

TRUMAN: The Lord calls His temple a "house of prayer" and teaches us to come there for "the offering up of your most holy desires unto me" (D&C 88:119; 95:16).

We can take our deepest concerns to the temple and spread them before the Lord and expect to come away lightened in both senses of the word: no longer carrying burdens of care and with an understanding of the course we should take. Have you felt such reassurance and solace?

Elder Franklin D. Richards said, "If occasion should require, if sorrow, affliction or distress overtake, we may go to the House of the Lord and find a panacea that can be found nowhere else for the ills of mortal life."[19] Seek this solace.

One day a sister in our ward commented on how beautiful our seventeen-year-old Emily was and how happy she was to see Emily each day at the Provo Temple open house. I didn't know what she meant. We had been there as a family on the first day of the temple open house, but I had no idea that every day from then until the dedication Emily had walked from the high school up to the temple, just to be there. When I asked her, "What did you do there? Why did you go each day?" she answered simply, "I went through the regular tour and then I would sit in the celestial room as long as they would let me—just to feel the presence of the Lord, to pray, to commune."

Have you ever felt like that? Have you been drawn to the temple like our Emily? Each day she would start for home but would end up in the temple. It was like a magnet to her. It was wonderfully habit-forming.

ANN: Feeling this closeness to the temple is not automatic, but it can be sought after, if we seek with all our hearts. "And ye shall seek me, and find me, when ye shall search for me with all your heart. And I will be found of you" (Jeremiah 29:13–14).

Little by little the Lord reveals Himself to us and in turn, we present ourselves to Him, revealing as much as we dare until we are able to lay it all before Him.

Let me tell you about a wonderful word in Hebrew which embodies our finally being able to open ourselves to the Lord. It is *Hin ani.* It is the common answer of prophets when the Lord calls them to be His messengers. Abraham said it. Samuel said it. Isaiah said it. It means, "Behold, here am I," with the implicit intent of "I am at your service, what will you have me do?" It is another way of saying, "Thy will be done." Christ said it first when He offered Himself in the heavenly council to do for us what we could not do for ourselves.

To open ourselves to the Lord entails risks and costs, because once we offer, we will be sent and we become responsible. But once we go, we are on His errand and He promises to bless us. He wants us to succeed—to return to Him. He weeps or rejoices over us just as we do over our children (see Moses 7:28–40).

So in the days ahead, when there is no other way to approach the Lord to tell Him what you are willing to give, just whisper *hinunee.* It is another way of saying, "Behold the handmaid of the Lord; be it unto me according to thy word" (Luke 1:38).

TRUMAN: Joseph Smith once said, speaking of our not asking enough or being thankful enough in our prayers: "We have not desired as much from the hand of the Lord through faith and obedience, as we ought to have done, yet we have enjoyed great blessings, and we are not so sensible of this as we should be."[20]

Sometimes in the temple we feel like we are praying in the Garden of Eden and life is all beauty and goodness. And sometimes it is as if we are praying in the Garden of Gethsemane, and it is too hard to bear. Either way, the temple is a retreat and a place of Christ's intensive care, where His rays come together in focus and peace. When we taste consolation in the temple, we will recognize it later as we kneel at home and seek to commune with Him there.

ANN: There is a window where I routinely pray. I have been watching spring come as I kneel there each day. The trees begin with a pale green fuzz and there are red and yellow tulips peeking up, sometimes through snow. One day I watched two deer nibbling on our flowers. One morning recently, as I prayed in this sacred place, all at once I realized that I was feeling precisely as I do in the temple. It was such an electric moment. It was almost as if I *was* in the temple. I had begun praying just before dawn. As I continued in prayer the sun suddenly came over the mountain. First its brightness dazzled me, even with my eyes closed, and then I felt its warmth. It took my breath away. It was such a ready symbol of God's presence.

I have been pondering lately about what *glory* means. "And the glory of the Lord shone round about" (D&C 76:19) or "I was clothed upon with glory."[21] Maybe we miss tiny bits of glory when we fail to notice sunrises and sunsets. I think I had a tiny glimpse of glory in that moment at my window. And the silence of the morning at first light was a necessary preparation. My mind was like a clean slate.

What about praying for each other? Joseph Smith taught the sisters in Nauvoo: "It grieves me that there is no fuller fellowship—if one member suffer all feel it. By union of feeling we obtain power with God."[22] Jesus said, "Be agreed as touching all things whatsoever ye ask of me" (D&C 27:18).

Recently I wrote to a friend who is seriously ill: "This morning we were in the Mount Timpanogos Temple and stood in that unique sacred circumstance to pray for you. How blessed we are to live in a time when we walk out of the world into such holy precincts and feel the glorious difference, and then reenter the world with the determination to keep the holiness with us."

My friend Shirley says she often prays for something while she is in the temple and receives her answer later, outside. So the temple becomes the channel through which our prayers ascend, and later we can access the answers somewhere else. I love that concept.

HOW DOES OUR LOVE FOR OUR FAMILIES AND THOSE WE SERVE EXPAND THROUGH TEMPLE WORSHIP?

TRUMAN: President Howard W. Hunter said that the purpose of the temple is to reunite the family of God.[23] He also said, "In the ordinances of the temple, the foundations of the eternal family are sealed in place."[24]

A dear friend of ours, Mary Finlayson, was asked to write about the Spirit of Elijah. She wrote: "I have spent the last four years in an effort to knit together my grandfather's unraveling family, and I have loved every minute of it. . . . I will never forget the feelings of family I had when they arrived at the Lion House [for our first family reunion]—feelings of love without conditions, complete belonging, and an overwhelming desire to serve each one in any way possible. . . . I don't know how it works but I suddenly saw why we are led by our prophets to do these things. I now believe that those feelings that surge up in us as we gather our earthly families [now living or gone ahead] are a type. At some point, if we continue to grow toward it, we will feel those same automatic feelings of sacrificial love toward everyone we encounter. In short, I think we're just practicing on our blood relations for the real thing. At some point, we will gaze at any face and recognize instantly our kinship, sprung from the same Father."[25]

ANN: What do you think about as you sit waiting for a temple session to begin? Once, as I sat bathed in the silence, I looked again at the name of the person for whom I had come. I felt a sudden kinship, though two hundred years separated us in time. I whispered in my heart to her through the thin veil: "Welcome to this beautiful temple, Sarah. I hope that you will love it as I do." Since that singular day when I sensed her reality, I try to reach out to the person for whom I am officiating. I tell her how I pray that she will accept the covenants and love them. I tell her how grateful I am that I can do this for her because it is such a blessed opportunity for me to ponder anew the wondrous truths that I have treasured for many years. There are many quiet moments throughout the endowment ceremony when no words are being spoken. In these times she will see the endowment with spirit eyes enlightened by her time in the spirit world. And I will search again, using all the capacity a body provides. I will inquire, "Lord, what do you have for me here today?" We will both have a unique opportunity through this sacred pattern to better understand godliness.

Even the arithmetic of our temple service teaches us. Only once do we receive our own endowment. From that moment, each time we enter the temple—hopefully hundreds of times—we enter to serve others. This is the pattern of Jesus, who reaches out to all of us as our Savior. In our small reaching, beyond ourselves to our families and those we serve, we can learn to become saviors on Mount Zion.

I heard a wonderful story of Gandhi that illustrates this transcendent giving principle, a more complete consecration. Gandhi was traveling on a slow-moving train in India when one of his sandals slipped off and tumbled down the embankment. One of his followers started to jump down to retrieve it as the train lumbered along, but Gandhi restrained him. He quickly unfastened the other sandal, tossing it beside the first so that whoever found it would have a pair. I want to learn to feel like that.

TRUMAN: The world assumes that our relatives are dead, gone, and indifferent to us. It is just the other way around. They are alive—perhaps in some ways more alive than we. They are close at hand and concerned about us.

Joseph Smith taught: "Enveloped in flaming fire, they are not far from us, and know and understand our thoughts, feelings, and motions, and are often pained therewith."[26]

Yes, and surely they rejoice with us as well. I can testify that as the air is thinner on high mountains, so the veil is thin in the temples of the Lord.

Our loved ones in the spirit world know what this life is like. They are not, the Prophet taught, "idle spectators."[27] They yearn over us. My good counselor in a stake presidency, James Harper, tells the story of a woman who was baptized as proxy for her mother, a mother who had been handicapped and terribly difficult to live with. Her daughter felt both healing and forgiveness in that process.

ANN: Our family shared a tender experience as we went to the temple to perform baptisms, endowments, and sealings for the family of my grandfather's uncle John Pearson. Before we took our grandchildren up to the temple to be baptized for the Pearson family, I read to them from my grandfather's missionary journal, which he kept while serving his mission in England. In his journal, he wrote of each member of that family and how he loved them and longed to bring them into the Church. We assigned each grandchild a name from these entries; they saw the people for whom they would be baptized through my grandfather's eyes.

The sunny morning when we went to the temple in behalf of that family was almost exactly one hundred years since my grandfather had written these things in his journal. I told our grandchildren that Grandfather Nicholls was a fine missionary who died shortly after his return home. Surely he had plenty of time in the spirit world to complete the teaching begun in 1894. As we went into the font area, some missionaries were just finishing but lingered to watch our family. Later they approached me and said, "We could feel the presence of the Pearson family as you did those baptisms. Thank you."

TRUMAN: As I stood waist-deep in the font, inviting my granddaughters and then grandsons to join me there, one by one, it all seemed like closing a circuit—like coming home. Perhaps I sensed a little of what Wilford Woodruff described in the St. George Temple; it was as if the baptismal room itself was charged. Swept up in the feeling, I wept and made a mistake in the wording, but was grateful to be kindly corrected. Later with my hands on still-moist heads I felt the blessing of conferring the gift of the Holy Ghost. It was not perfunctory. It was reality.

ANN: As we were leaving the temple I pointed out the bas-relief of the Samaritan woman at the well with Jesus. It is on the far wall in the waiting room of the Provo Temple, so our grandchildren had to peek inside to see it. I asked them, not having any idea what they would answer, "Why do you think they have that story in the temple?" I had nothing particular in mind. Instantly, one of those guileless, intrepid souls spoke right up: "Because Jesus is telling her who He is and that's what happens in the temple. He tells us who He really is."

TRUMAN: God unites us by love. Satan's whole work is to separate and isolate us by discord, anger, hate, and the clamor for rights. All of us know what isolation feels like. We need to know what the unity of love feels like. I believe that it is impossible to feel the Spirit of the Lord and not feel love. And perhaps vice versa. When we know what love feels like we cannot help loving others. Love is contagious.

ANN: We all have moments when we feel as if no one loves us. "Nobody loves me, nobody understands, nobody cares." But in the temple it is different. God's gentle, unfailing love fills His house. We can access it there: we can open ourselves to God's love as His children. Christ cares for us precisely because He participated in what we are going through. He yearns to gather us under His wings and nourish us, to "encircle [us] in the arms of [His] love" (D&C 6:20; 3 Nephi 10:4).

Temple workers themselves contribute to this feeling of love and caring. I remember entering the Frankfurt Germany Temple. The man at the recommend desk, whose gray hair and lined face showed he had survived World War II, extended his hand to shake mine as he said, "Velcome to the house of the Lord." I wept as I sensed the reality of entering God's own house.

TRUMAN: Do you think those who are in the temple every day feel that love in a special way? Do they feel it constantly? We heard a fine temple president, Elder Carlos E. Asay, and his wife explain their view. President Asay spoke of the endowment as an "exchange of love." God loves us enough to give us commandments and make covenants with us that will inspire and can ultimately exalt us. Keeping covenants keeps us from sinning. We should be willing to honor the trust extended in eternal covenants by keeping them. Is this not "an exchange of love"? he asked.

ANN: What a touching moment it was for me when a dear friend confided about a year after her husband's death, "He adored me." Then, weeping, she continued, "Now nobody feels that way about me anymore." I could feel some of her devastation. All I knew to say was, "The Lord loves you deeply. Pray to feel *that* love in His house."

President Asay also taught us, "The temple is the bridge between heaven and earth—the seen and the unseen—and the bridge is love." We feel such love for the Lord Jesus Christ, who pleads our cause before our Father. I know He truly loves me. He truly loves you. The Spirit helps communicate that love.

TRUMAN: Such love is a taste of immortality. As Elder Parley P. Pratt wrote, the Spirit "develops beauty of person, form and features."[28] A sensitive temple worker once shared with me a glimpse of this ultimate blessing. He had officiated in the presence of many aged and infirm and arthritic couples as they performed sealings. He felt admiration but also sympathy for their slow-moving, patient labor. Then he suddenly saw them as they would be in the resurrection. He could hardly find words: "They were exquisite . . . splendid . . . youthful . . . lovely."

TRUMAN: Elder Henry B. Eyring told of a mother who was driving down a freeway hardly able to see through her tears. She had just visited her son, a convicted murderer, in prison. "Why, why?" she cried out. "Why am I the mother of such a son?" And a voice from on high replied, "Because you are the only one on this planet who will go on loving him."[29]

There are ways, too deep and poignant to describe, that the Lord's temple service can reach the hardest of cases, bring faith to the faithless and hope to the hopeless. Christ teaches in holy places that He never gives up. Neither should we.

ANN: Covenants bind us by love. Elder Henry B. Eyring once said that he had been taught that covenants were like a business contract, in which one person agrees to do something and the other agrees to do something else in return. But after serious reflection, he felt something new, something more powerful about our covenants with God. Covenant keeping is not a cold business deal but a warm relationship, bound by love.

Elder Eyring explained: "The Lord, with whom I am blessed to have made covenants, loves me and you with a steadfastness about which I continually marvel and which I want with all my heart to emulate." He went on to say, "We are blessed by the Abrahamic covenant, and we are bound by it. But we are not bound by compulsion. We are bound by his love for us and by the love He evokes in us."[30]

All other virtues spring from this Christlike love. We forgive, we have mercy, we have empathy, we are willing to lift and bless and help when we are filled with that love. How can we give in to anger or impatience when our hearts are brimming with love? No wonder the scripture cries out, "Pray . . . with all the energy of heart, that ye may be filled with this love" (Moroni 7:48). We can pray daily for that sweet selflessness. Charity never stops, never fails. It reaches back to us even from beyond the veil.

HOW DO WE TAKE THE TEMPLE HOME WITH US, AND HOW CAN THE TEACHINGS OF THE TEMPLE TRANSFORM OUR HOMES?

TRUMAN: We've had the privilege of attending three temple dedications, two with our family. The latest was the Mount Timpanogos Utah Temple dedication, which we attended with a whole row of our children and their children. As the services progressed, we looked across that row and saw their upturned faces as they sang "The Spirit of God Like a Fire Is Burning." At the conclusion we overheard Max, then age ten, whisper to his mother, "Thanks for bringing me here!" We were knit closely that day. We were one. We remembered that President Lorenzo Snow instructed little children to give the Hosannah Shout at the top of their lungs because that would be the way they would greet Jesus Christ at His Second Coming.[31]

ANN: Our homes can, like the temple, be holy sanctuaries in this far-from-holy world. Bruce Hafen, when he was provost at BYU, described the world today as a polluted river. We are like fish swimming in the pollution, often carried by a current of which we are only vaguely aware, until someone swims against the current. Then we see the contrast.[32]

The Lord has commanded us: "Behold, it is my will, that all they who call on my name, and worship me according to mine everlasting gospel, should gather together, and stand in holy places" (D&C 101:22).

How is a Zion built? By producing and gathering the "pure in heart." Eliza R. Snow learned from the Prophet that the curse on the earth would not be lifted all at once, but that each time we dedicate a temple we lift the curse a little. Our homes can be the mini-temples, the points of light that will recreate a little bit of heaven on earth leading to the Millennium. All of us are "homemakers." We make a home wherever we eat and sleep. There are several things we can do to help make our homes holy.

TRUMAN: We can help make our homes holy by dedicating them. Ann and I have painted, fixed up, shined, and then dedicated each of our homes. We were really dedicating ourselves to the purposes of the Lord in our family. We even dedicated our temporary apartment in Jerusalem. All the things we say, the prayers we offer, the blessings that are given, the feelings we experience—both good and bad—accumulate in our homes and are felt by those who come there. We add something to the sum each day. That's a sobering thought.

ANN: We can help make our homes holy by setting priorities. Family is first. Someone must be primarily responsible for dividing the tasks that keep a home going—no matter how many machines we have to cut down our work. We can't all abdicate everything. Orderliness, cleanliness, music, social life, decor—the abundant life is far different from merely existing in a space together. Someone or ones *must* have that as a priority or it will never happen.

Is home a place of beauty? Is home just a place to eat and sleep? Is there no lovely corner to curl up in to read a book? If spring is lagging outdoors, can we bring it inside with a pot of daisies or daffodils on the table for dinner—not for company but just because it's spring? If family is first, then shouldn't there be flowers for family? You will notice the temple grounds are alive with beauty. So can our homes be.

TRUMAN: We can help make our homes holy by creating order and fixed points to count on.

In the temple we learn a planned sequence. Do we have such fixed points in our home regimen? When do we sit together and share? Everyone in the family can count on family home evening as a fixed point in their week for planning family events and simply to celebrate being together.

ANN: What about dinnertime? Let's dine together! What a novel idea! Before you say, "Our family just can't," think about it. There is such an emphasis on good nutrition these days. We fill our freezers with well-balanced meals in individual, dated packets and then run in all directions, leaving each person to heat a nutritious meal in the microwave and eat it on the run all alone. Isn't nursing our babies a type that should teach us something? We have to do that together. From infancy to adulthood, we communicate through food. Dinner is a time to share. It's a time for bonding. It's an informal temple preparation class.

TRUMAN: We had a fixed point at our house that worked for us—5:30 P.M. was inviolate. Everyone worked around it. That was our family's daily appointment to eat dinner together; that was when we had family prayer; that was when we read the scriptures and were spiritually fed. But I think what we all remember best was that we talked. We did not let the urgent rob us of this important time together.

We can help make our homes holy by living what we've learned in the temple. When we keep our temple covenants, they help us to cheerfully, patiently reverence one another at home. We become sanctifying influences to each other and all who come there. We quietly learn to live celestially, like Christ, creating a little bit of heaven on earth. Patience and prayer are part of the process.

ANN: When the Provo Temple was to be dedicated, we made plans to prepare our family for what we anticipated as a once-in-a-lifetime experience. We had a series of family home evenings focusing on the temple: one honoring our ancestors; one celebrating our wedding day, complete with photo album, ring, the story of our courtship, and so on; one explaining what we could of the activities that would go on in the temple. The culmination was a family visit to the temple open house—the first time our children would actually be able to enter the Lord's house with us. In preparation we each bathed carefully, washed our hair, put on all clean Sunday clothes, and drove to the temple. We explained to our children that this kind of cleanliness was part of the symbolism of purity which is essential for entering the presence of the Lord in His house.

TRUMAN: We learned an unexpected lesson from this experience. We arrived at an empty parking lot. There we were, all scrubbed, clean, excited, and expectant. But the door was locked; it was a Monday. What a letdown. But the lights were all on so I went to look inside, pressing my nose against the glass. There was the temple president, showing his own family through the temple. Seeing us, and having compassion, he invited us to join them. We knew for a moment how it felt to be denied entrance to the temple. And just as suddenly, we experienced more joy than we had prayed and planned for.

ANN: Our homes can become holy places and still be lived in. They can be clean, orderly, and reverent—within the parameters of keeping happy, growing children in them.

As a grandmother I remember the first time the whole family came for Thanksgiving dinner to our newly remodeled house. The paint was fresh, and there was not a mark on any wall. I had foolishly hoped to preserve its pristine appearance for a week or two. As they all left, I gasped at little muddy footprints that ran the length of the new silver gray carpet and handprints on the walls and windows and mirrors. My newly clean home! But then I caught myself. I've learned to cherish fingerprints.

TRUMAN: Orson Pratt gives us a wonderful vision of glorified homes in the future: "In the latter days there will be a people so pure in Mount Zion, with a house established upon the tops of the mountains, that God will manifest himself, not only in their Temple . . . [but] when they retire to their [homes], behold each [home] will be lighted up by the glory of God—a pillar of flaming fire by night."[33]

CONCLUSION

TRUMAN: We have spoken of the ideal, the vision. It may seem remote, distant, even utterly beyond us. But we can have a foretaste in this world. As Joseph Smith admonished, "Let these truths sink down in our hearts, that we may even here begin to enjoy that which shall be in full hereafter."[34]

Ponder these confirming words in a letter to a remarkable woman, Eliza R. Snow, from Apostle Wilford Woodruff. The letter was written fifteen years after she became a widow, and thirty years before her death. Note the sense of fulfilled promises and the allusions to the temple:

"Thy soul hath been inspired with the spirit of God, and eternal light and truth. . . . Thy lamp hath been lit at God's holy altar where the oil was pure and the spirit free so thou couldst weigh eternal truth. . . .

"Thy words and testimony will live and speak in flames of holy fire . . . long after thou art with thy Father in heaven clothed with immortality and crowned with light. Thy garments are clear of the blood of all men. Thy soul is as pure as the crystal stream that flows from its snowy bed. Thou hast been true and faithful and art sealed unto eternal life and secured unto thyself a crown of glory. No power shall take it. It awaits thy coming. Ah, what joy!"[35]

ANN: No wonder Eliza could say to the women of her day and to us, "We are women of God, women fulfilling high and responsible positions, performing sacred duties."[36]

We finish with the invitation with which we began: Come, let us go up to the temple where the Lord will teach us of His ways, and we will walk in His paths until we have learned them (see Isaiah 2:3).

Jesus moved from grace to grace to become more and more. And when a sick sinner asked, "Lord, if thou wilt, thou canst make me clean," He replied, "I will; be thou clean" (Matthew 8:2–3). We, too, can be made whole. The temple is absolutely necessary for that to happen in our lives. It is the finishing of our faith. It is the crowning of our lives on earth. It is the only place on earth where our families can be knit together, bound by a love which Jesus has demonstrated once and for all in the Atonement.

In that holy house we can see ourselves as we really are; we can find Jesus Christ and understand who He really is; we can understand a new level of purity and learn to pray with power. As we search the teachings we receive, we will know how to overcome the devil and, ultimately, how to part the veil.[37] The temple is the bridge of love between this world and the next.

May we invite you with the words of Isaiah: "O house of Jacob, come ye, and let us walk in the light of the Lord"—the sunshine of His love (Isaiah 2:5).

I have tried to describe my feelings about the temple in the following lines:

> *In the temple*
> *The quiet closes round me*
> *like fog.*

God's house reverberates
with silence,
filled with echoes
from the faithful
who have followed the light
to here, like a star.
White, we come clothed in white
to this place,
of radiant light.
Dear Host
of this Heavenly House,
if I come,
clothed in the pure white
of a new lamb,
with my heart as new,
may I, too,
be lighted?

6

ELIJAH AND THE
TURNING OF HEARTS

There is something in the scriptures about an offering to be offered up one day by some specific persons, namely the sons of Levi (see D&C 13:1). Puzzlement. Who are they? What is the offering?

In early 1847 Brigham Young was ill at a place called Winter Quarters. He had been prayerful and his feelings were mixed. He still was deeply grieved at the loss of his closest earthly friend, Joseph Smith, and was burdened heavily with the kingdom and its leadership. He was puzzled over the question of adoption. Some of the Saints, whose own literal forebears showed a lack of interest or even deep hostility regarding the Church, wished these forebears could be grafted into a faithful family. Some such ordinances were performed. So Brother Brigham prayed about it.

He had a dream in which he saw the Prophet Joseph Smith. Some beautiful passages demonstrate that Brother Brigham wanted to join the Prophet. If you think that wasn't sincere and lasting, you should know that his last words on earth, thirty years later, would be one word three times repeated—"Joseph, Joseph, Joseph."[1]

After this 1847 interchange and the assurance the Prophet there gave him that he must live on, Brigham inquired about adoption, and the Prophet replied. In the account there are seven different ways in which he said, "Tell the people to be sure to get and keep the Spirit of the Lord."[2]

There is a marvelous statement about how we know the spirit received is the Spirit of the Lord, for Joseph said at one point: "They can tell the Spirit of the Lord from all other spirits; it will whisper peace and joy to their souls; it will take malice, hatred, strife and all evil from their hearts; and their whole desire will be to do good, bring forth righteousness and build up the kingdom of God." Then the interesting conclusion: "Be sure to tell the people to keep the Spirit of the Lord; and if they will, they will find themselves just as they were organized by our Father in Heaven before they came into the world. Our Father in Heaven organized the human family [in the premortal councils], but they are all disorganized and in great confusion."[3] Such was Brigham Young's glimpse of the crucial nature of the Spirit in finding ourselves united in a family relationship.

It could be said that the earliest and latest revelations in the Doctrine and Covenants touch on this theme, the first being section 2 (which was actually given before section 1). That is the revelation or statement of Moroni to the Prophet Joseph Smith in 1823. It says that Elijah will be sent. And what for? To "plant in the hearts of the children the promises made to the fathers, and the hearts of the children shall turn to their fathers" (JS–H 1:39). (Elijah will be among those who participate in the most glorious family reunion in all history. It could be called a sacramental wedding breakfast to be held following the Lord's Second Coming [see D&C 27:5–14].)

Elijah did come. He came to the Kirtland Temple on April 3, 1836 (see D&C 110:13–16). Jewish literature is replete with the promise and expectation of Elijah's coming. That is the last promise of the Old Testament, in the last verses of Malachi. And it is Jewish tradition that on the second night of Passover they must leave open the door and place at the table head an empty chair and a goblet full of wine in the expectation that Elijah may come. It is interesting, especially in light of that Jewish tradition, that April 3, 1836, was the second day of Passover. The symbolism is beautiful. Elijah came, as they expect, to a home—the Lord's home. He came to a goblet of wine—the sacramental wine. He came to turn hearts, which is more than changing minds—he turns hearts to hearts. He somehow bridges some gap, some alienation, some separation that has occurred in the human family.

No subject preoccupied the Prophet Joseph Smith more than this one. In his later years he spoke at least eight times pleading with the Saints to ponder and pray over this principle. We ordinarily say that Elijah did something pertaining to the dead or work for the dead—a half truth. In the first place, no one is really dead. Those who are in the spirit world are in some ways more alive than some of us here. For instance, Elder Melvin J. Ballard said that they have every feeling "intensified" spiritually.[4] And as for their being dead and gone, no, they are not gone either. The prophets teach us that the spirit world is not in some remote galaxy; it is here, it is near. And as the Prophet put it, speaking of their feelings for us—those righteous souls who are bound to us somehow by the anxieties of their forebearing—"their bowels yearn over us."[5] He said they "are not idle spectators" in the last days.[6]

So Elijah does have something to do with them. But the Prophet taught that he also has something to do with us, with the living. Had he not come, the whole earth would be cursed; or, in another version, the earth would be utterly wasted at Christ's coming (D&C 2:2–3; JS–H 1:39). Wasted, I take it, means at least two things. It would be in a sense a waste if this earth, created by our Father and His Son as the dwelling place of their family, turned out to be a house barren—not a home, not a place of genuine familial love. In that sense it would have been a waste to create it. But second, were there not a family welded and united and full of love for Christ, it would be the case that all mankind, unable to endure His presence, would be laid waste at His coming. Thank God for the restoration of the power to prepare such a family. That conferral came through Elijah.

The Prophet said, speaking of this subject, "How shall God come to the rescue of this generation?" And he answered, "He will send Elijah."[7]

That generation may have been a difficult one, but this generation in which you and I live is in some ways a worse one. Constantly students around the country ask me, "Do you think the world is getting better or worse?" And I always answer, "Yes." The wheat is getting "wheatier" and the tares are getting "tarier"— and rapidly.

How can a prophet change a whole generation, and an ancient prophet at that? We can know a few things about Elijah. Know that his name is interesting—*El-i-yah:* literally, in Hebrew, "My God is Jehovah." But his name also symbolizes the sealing or the union of father and son. Know that he conferred keys, and we understand, if only dimly, that that means authority—priesthood authority. There are men on the earth today who hold those keys by direct line of ordination. Every marriage in this Church that is binding both here and hereafter has been performed under those keys and their delegated authority.

Further, Elijah had a revelatory function. There is a spirit that is somehow emanating through him and his work and ministry that has reached out far beyond the bounds of this Church, turning hearts and not just heads. And one account says that it was his function to reveal to us "the covenants of the fathers in relation to the children, and the covenants of the children in relation to the fathers"[8]—perhaps pointing to something that happened prior to mortality.

Elijah is also an exemplar of what is his mission, for it is not yet over. As a translated being, one not yet subject to death, he had the unique privilege of ministering to the Master and the three chief Apostles on the Mount of Transfiguration (see Matthew 17:1–8) in an experience which we are told we cannot yet fully understand, the fulness of the account having been reserved for the future.

A Jewish apocalyptic tradition says that those two prophets who are to one day testify in the streets of Jerusalem to prepare the hearts of the Jews to be turned to the prophets (see D&C 98:16–17) and are then to literally be killed and lie in the streets—martyrs just prior to the coming of the Messiah—are Elijah and Enoch. Elijah has been patient through millennia awaiting the opportunity to bring earth and heaven back together, to tie together the old and new worlds, to take the estranged and the alienated and the embittered and somehow transform their hearts, and to prepare all of the family who are willing to be family, welding them indissolubly in order to greet the Christ.

Let us draw a few personal and emotional implications from this. Feeling, after all, centers in the heart, and this is not a matter of mere intellect. It is a matter of feeling something inside. The

Prophet said on one occasion to the Relief Society that he grieved that they were not exhibiting greater union of feeling among themselves. And he went on to say, "By union of feeling we obtain power with God."[9] And repeatedly the Lord has said in modern revelation that He reveals himself by His Spirit to the mind and the heart: "Behold, I will tell you in your mind and in your heart by the Holy Ghost, which shall come upon you and which shall dwell in your heart" (D&C 8:2). This is an impressive blending of intellect and sentiment.

We need not dwell on the point that in our culture the family is coming unglued. There are those who hold that the great wave of the future, a better future as they see it, is to totally abandon the notion of united families—and they recommend it. One can call attention to devastating statistics outside the Church, but I want to talk strictly about what is happening inside it. One of our statistics, and I am only approximating, is that there are well over 600,000 children in this Church who are being raised by single parents. There are delinquent fathers. There are delinquent children. Just from conversation in my own office over the years on the BYU campus I have heard sentences that tell it all. For example: "My mother gave me five hundred dollars and told me to go away." Or, "I couldn't possibly tell my father. He would kill me." Or again, "My mother has been divorced three times." Or again, "No one in my family cares anything for the Church." Or again, "Just before I left for my mission my father threatened to take my life." Or again, "I don't dare go home."

Robert Frost saw clearly the meaning of home. He said: "Home is the place where, when you have to go there, / They have to take you in."[10] Would that it were so. Many who are joining the Church in this generation are doing so at the cost of never being permitted through that door of home again. My own great-grandfather wrote a letter from Nauvoo. He was a squire—a kind of amateur attorney—who had loved the Mormon people but had never joined them. And his motivation was elementary: he had a wife and a son, and both of them said that if he ever did join the Mormons, that would be the end; they would never speak to him again. The letter to Brigham Young said, "Is this what the Lord requires of me?" And Brigham Young's answer, in a word, was "yes." My great-grandfather joined the Church, and his wife and his son kept their word.

Yes, we are in a real world. And the alienation, the pain, the hostility, the torment, the trauma, even in some Latter-day Saint homes, is a long distance from Elijah, who said he would turn hearts toward and not away. Is there hope? There is.

Let's discuss now not what one needs to do but what one needs to feel. First there is forgiveness. We are glib, I think, in quoting the passages that talk about our needing to forgive, and even to forgive all people. They are there. One of the strongest passages concerns the Prophet Joseph pleading with his brethren to forgive him of his weaknesses. And then it goes on to say that if they don't forgive him, there remains in them the greater sin (see D&C 64:9). That is strong language, saying that one's refusal to forgive a sinner is a worse sin than whatever sin the sinner has committed. But forgiveness is the very nature of Christ's way.

I suggest that it may be difficult to forgive your enemies, but it is even more difficult to forgive your loved ones who have sometimes manifested hate—and you have to forgive them in response. It is harder to forgive your loved ones, because you care about them and you have to go on living with them, or struggling to, and they can go on hurting you over the years and the decades. But our hearts will never turn to our fathers in the way this spirit of which we have been testifying motivates us to do unless we forgive.

You see, we have inherited all kinds of things. There is a standard procedure for students with bad report cards. They can go home and say, "Look, Mom," or "Look, Dad. Which do you think it is, heredity or environment?" And their parents can say, "Neither of the above." The fact is that we willingly chose to come into the world, likely in this time and circumstance. When a young person says to his parents in deepest animosity, "I didn't ask to be born," if the parents give the proper, prophetic answer they will say: "Oh, yes, you did. You not only asked for it, you prepared for it, trained for it, were reserved for it." Both child and parent are mutually involved.

And by the way, that's a "snarl" word in our generation: *Involved.* No one wants to get involved, in anything. Instead they say, Do your own thing. Be yourself. But you and I and all of us are involved. It was collusion between us all. And therefore, as you look back at your seventy or so forebears—that's what it would take, at fifty years each, only seventy generations to get you back to Abraham—you might recognize that you have inherited the blood of many generations. And *blood* may not be a correct word scientifically, but in the scriptures it stands for *seed,* which means heredity, the inheritance of tendencies, and all of us have them. You have the blood of this generation, from which we must become clean—"clean from the blood of this generation" (D&C 88:85). If you do, you will be clean from the blood of every generation, because it is compounded and accumulated into now—and that includes the blood of some degeneration.

So perhaps you do have problems that you can blame on your ancestors, and if you forgive that and choose to stand close to the Lord in the process of purifying your life, that will affect your whole family in both directions. You are not alone. There is no way you can gain solitary and neutral ground. You are in it—you are involved. And this, I believe, is one of the profound meanings of that long, laborious allegory in the book of Jacob, the allegory of the tame and wild olive trees. If you take a wild branch and graft it into a tame one, if the branch is strong enough it will eventually corrupt and spoil the tree all the way to the roots. But if you take a tame branch and graft it in to a wild tree, in due time, if that branch is strong enough, it will heal and regenerate to the very roots. You will then have been an instrument in the sanctification even of your forebears.

Do these considerations ever sober us in moments when we suppose either that no one cares for us or that whether they care or not, our life makes no difference? To be that kind of branch and achieve that kind of transformation backward and forward is perhaps the greatest achievement of this world. But to do it one must be great, one must be linked, bound to the Lord Jesus Christ. One must be mighty. One must be something of a savior. And that is exactly what the Prophet Joseph Smith said we are: "saviors on Mount Zion."[11] And how are we to be saviors on Mount Zion? he asked once in a discourse. He answered by saying that we do so by first building, then going into the temples of the Lord and, in our own first-person presence, going through all the temple ordinances for and in behalf of loved ones who have passed on. This can "redeem them that they may . . . be exalted to thrones of glory." And it will help fulfill "the mission of Elijah."[12] Yes, we can be saviors, redeemers of our families.

We have many examples in our history. I chose this one not because it is exceptional but because it isn't. Erastus Snow, given a blessing by Patriarch Joseph Smith Sr., was told in effect: "Brother Erastus, your father knows nothing of the gospel of Jesus

Christ, but the Lord God will be your father and He will watch over you. And if you will walk in the full path of righteousness, the time will come when you will be saved with your kindred flesh; and in due time, if you are worthy, these blessings which I pronounce upon you will be confirmed upon you by your own father. And then your joy will be full."[13]

The capacity to forgive comes only through the capacity for loving the Lord Jesus Christ. And He taught us how. He said, "Pray for your enemies." That's different, I remind you, from praying against your enemies. If you want to know how you can turn feelings of hostility into feelings of forgiveness and love, that's how. You pray for them. You may choke in the effort, but as you keep going, the time comes when you mean it. And then you not only mean that you want to forgive, and feel it, but you even find yourself praying that He will forgive. And you look with compassion instead of spite at the whole traditional mix that has made you what you are and to some degree what you aren't.

Along with forgiveness, there is something we must do that is even harder. The word is *sacrifice.* And we know that the family of man was taught from Adam down to make external sacrifice with the firstlings of the flock, the firstborn. These were consumed, burned on an altar, all to typify and prepare for the coming of the living sacrifice, who was Christ Himself. We now know that when the Lord appeared to the Nephites He said, in substance: "No longer will I accept burnt offerings. From now on I will accept only your hearts. You must bring to me the sacrifice of a broken heart and a contrite spirit" (see 3 Nephi 9:19–20).

We usually use the term "broken heart" to mean being radically hurt in a romance. That meaning is accepted, but in the scriptural usage a broken heart is a malleable, meltable, moveable heart, and a contrite spirit is an honest, acknowledging spirit that

86

says, "I am, in fact, dependent on what I am in fact dependent on." There is not self-deprecation here, only honesty: "I need help." And when that is acknowledged, help comes.

I suggest that one sacrifice the sons of Levi and the daughters of Levi are to offer in the end is the willingness to give themselves in the cause of saviorhood and to care more about family and the preservation and intensification of family than they care about anything else in this world. That has costs. Some things have to be given up. Some things have to be postponed. So the focus is sacrifice.

I have to say honestly that I believe it is painful. I have to say I believe that there are many among us who are easily pulled in other directions. And I have to say I consider that a tragedy. I occasionally hear housewives say that they are "mere housewives." What have you done in the last twenty years? Oh, nothing—just fed my family three meals a day and more or less kept them together. Is that all? President Lorenzo Snow said with power on one occasion that if a woman raised a righteous family she "ought to be saved if she never does another good thing." [14] Our generation is making attractive every other thing but family. That is not the gospel of Jesus Christ.

So I plead with you, be forgiving and be sacrificing.

Flying in from the Far East some time ago, I found on the plane a young man obviously recognizable as a Mormon elder. We chatted. And I soon learned that his father had died while he was on his mission. When I was myself a mission president, I prayed every night and every morning for two things: one, that I would not have to send any missionary—male or female—home in disgrace, and two, that I would not have to send an elder or a sister home dead. In a way that's an unfair prayer, because I suspect that, with tens of thousands of young people out in the real world, in the long run there is no way to avoid some such tragedies. But I so prayed. I had not foreseen another difficulty, and that was to have to call in a missionary and tell him that one or the other of his parents—or in one case both—were gone.

This elder on the plane had lost his father, who had not been particularly faithful in the Church. His mother had taken up the burden and of course, as required, had sent the monthly check. As I got off the plane, and I was first off, I saw a face and something told me that this was his mother. I went to a position where I could see both her face and his. He got off and walked along a bit casually, carrying cameras and briefcase. And then he saw her. There was recognition, gratitude, forgiveness for whatever may have been amiss in the past, and a total royal embrace. That's it. That's everything.

It is precisely that kind of embrace and reunion that you and I were sent into the world to make possible with loved ones in a future existence. It will not be possible except if we are repentant and have faith in the Lord Jesus Christ sufficient to enable us to forgive and to sacrifice. That is our mission and our commission.

Occasionally when I have been in Jerusalem I have tried in my weakness to picture what He promises us will happen there one day. Mount Olivet, or the Mount of Olives, is the place from which He ascended. It is the place of His greatest suffering. It is the place where there was a garden, *Gat shemen* (Hebrew for "Garden of the Oil Press"), where, as it were, He trod the olive press to produce the oil of healing, the balm, the peace.

That place today, if you study it carefully, is a place of everything except reunion. It is a place of destruction. Graves are everywhere. Shattered things are everywhere. Barbed wire, glass, the droppings of animals, everything you can name. And hostility and bitterness are symbolized on that very mount in the fact that different faiths, each with its own claim, build churches, build basilicas, and then each refuses to acknowledge the existence of the others. There are machine-gun remnants. There is a monument to a place where paratroopers in the Six-Day War were gunned down by the dozens. War is what is symbolized there.

Yet the promise of the Lord Jesus Christ is that He will descend to that mount (see D&C 45:48). His foot will touch it. It will then cleave in twain, and there will be an earthquake. Dramatic, but true—an earthquake covering the whole earth. And there will be a transformation of the earth, preparing it for its terrestrial condition. As He descends with His worthy hosts, the privilege will also be given to those righteous who remain here to be caught up together to meet Him. We will not have to simply remain and wait, but, as in every genuine demonstration of true love, we will want to take our own steps toward the full embrace.

Thus it is our privilege and calling to become in our own limited way redemptors of the human family, ours and His. It is impossible to love Him truly and not love what is His; and God assigned Him to all of us. And it is not possible for us to really love ourselves unless we love what is truly us, and that is the whole house of Israel to which we belong. As we learn to do this and accordingly act as saviors, we will be helping to fulfill the great mission of Elijah.

7

PURPOSES OF THE TEMPLE

In the century and a half since the dedication of the Kirtland
Temple, a profound heritage of temple consciousness has grown
in our midst. We all wish to drink more deeply of the fountain.
We are counseled over and over that this depends upon us, upon
our own spiritual preparation, our own probing and pondering
and praying. No one presumes to be our teacher. We are taught
to seek divine teaching. Joseph Smith said, "The best way to
obtain truth and wisdom is not to ask it from books, but to go to
God in prayer, and obtain divine teaching."[1]

TEN PURPOSES OF THE TEMPLE

In searching the counsels of our leaders, Stephen Covey and I
have distilled ten concrete assurances concerning the meaning of
temple worship that can give our quest some focus.

1. "The temples," said Elder John A. Widtsoe, "are the con-
servators of the great truths of the gospel."[2] Temple ordinances are

so packed, so freighted with the riches of celestial truth, that "only a fool" would attempt to unravel it into prosaic restatement. "We live in a world of symbols. No man or woman can come out of the temple endowed as he should be, unless he has seen, beyond the symbol, the mighty realities for which the symbols stand."[3] It is a "house of learning" (D&C 109:8) where we may be taught not only the vital truths of life in the setting of eternal life, but those "hidden treasures" (D&C 89:19) which are reserved for the faithful and which, as President Harold B. Lee testified, can be known even more powerfully in the heart than in the head.[4] From the beginning the Prophet taught that all these temple insights are "always governed by the principle of revelation,"[5] but also that even "the least Saint" may receive them "as fast as he is able to bear them."[6] What can emerge is wisdom—knowledge applied to decision.

2. The temple is a kind of observatory, as Hugh Nibley has written, built "boxed to the compass," a place designed for us to get "our bearings" on the universe and our own lives.[7] Elder George F. Richards spoke of the temple as "a measuring rod" by which we may over and over find our way through the struggles and confusions of our mortal journey and our individual missions.[8]

3. The temple is a house of prayer, of fasting and prayer, and for "the offering up of your most holy desires unto me" (D&C 95:16). It is therefore a place to take our family perplexities and needs. Like the malignant demon of which Christ spoke as He descended from the mount, some of our weak and sinful habits may be the kind that can only be overcome through prayer and fasting (Matthew 17:21).[9] Elder Widtsoe said that any of us "can solve his problems better and more quickly in the house of the Lord than anywhere else,"[10] and this view was shared by his wife.

Elder Melvin J. Ballard added, "When in the sacred walls of these buildings, while you are entitled to the Spirit of the Lord, and in the silent moments, the answer will come."[11]

4. Temples are places of covenant and promise, out of which come discernment, sensitizing us to true and false influences. The Lord refers to the temple as a sanctuary where He may "endow [us] with power from on high" (D&C 38:32; 95:8; 105:11, 33; 109:35). Thus, "our temples give us power—a power based on enlarged knowledge and intelligence—a power from on high, of a quality with God's own power."[12] We are to receive these blessings, Joseph Smith taught, "in order that you may be prepared and able to overcome all things."[13] Our covenants are, as President Harold B. Lee wrote, "an embodiment or an unfolding of the covenants each person should have assumed at baptism."[14] They are "calculated to unite our hearts, that we may be one in feeling and sentiment."[15] By union of feeling we obtain power with the heavens. The covenants confer upon us the "armor of God," a protection which, wrote Joseph Fielding Smith, "a man who does not go to the temple does not have."[16] Thus the temple is a fortress—there we withdraw from the world in order to return fortified to the struggle.

5. Temples are places of nourishment. From the days of the ancient temple of Solomon, sacred tradition teaches, the temple is, or is built upon, the very "navel of the universe,"[17] our link with all creative powers. Joseph was commanded to pray at Kirtland that through the temple we might "grow up in thee, and receive a fulness of the Holy Ghost, and be organized according to thy laws [celestial laws], and be prepared to obtain every needful thing" (D&C 109:15). Our "growing up" involves nurture in the surroundings of the divine life. It centers in Him who is the Life. He has promised, "I will manifest myself to my people in mercy in

this house" (D&C 110:7). "Most of all things," wrote Elder Franklin D. Richards, "I desire the Holy Spirit which giveth life, yea, life more abundantly of both body and spirit."[18] This enlivening power, which we are commanded to seek with our whole souls, not only gives us flashes of pure intelligence to meet our strains; it "quickens" us so that we live on a new level, in a new ocean, as it were.

6. The temple is "the house of the Lord." All the pure in heart who come into it shall see God.

"It is a great promise that to the temples God will come," wrote Elder John A. Widtsoe, "and that in them man shall see God. What does this promised communion mean? Does it mean that once in a while God may come into the temples, and that once in a while the pure in heart may see God there; or does it mean the larger thing, that the pure in heart who go into the temples, may, there, by the Spirit of God, always have a wonderfully rich communion with God? I think that is what it means to me and to you and to most of us. We have gone into these holy houses, with our minds freed from the ordinary earthly cares, and have literally felt the presence of God. In this way, the temples are always places where God manifests himself to man and increases his intelligence. A temple is a place of revelation."[19]

7. Temples are, as Elder Joseph Fielding Smith wrote, "places for sanctification."[20] The presence of and ordination to the priesthood and ultimately the fulness of the priesthood are there. (The Prophet Joseph Smith instructed: "Go to and finish the temple, and God will fill it with power, and you will then receive more knowledge concerning this priesthood."[21]) To receive knowledge of the priesthood is one thing. To receive the priesthood itself is another. Both are a privilege of the temple. As we magnify our callings—which are epitomized in the home—then, according to

promise, we are "sanctified by the Spirit unto the renewing of [our] bodies" (D&C 84:33). Perhaps this is the meaning of Elder John A. Widtsoe's statement that "no other Church requirement lifts man to a nearer likeness of the Lord."[22]

8. "The endowment," Joseph Smith taught, "was to prepare the disciples for their missions unto the world."[23] At Kirtland he prayed that "from this place they may bear exceedingly great and glorious tidings, in truth, unto the ends of the earth" (D&C 109:23). We think of this as extending the message of the gospel in missionary roles. That clearly includes teaching at home. We should carry the spirit of the temple into our homes to qualify, intensify, and enliven our efforts to grasp teaching moments with our children and with each other. It is a place where we are to be "instructed more perfectly" in order that we may instruct more perfectly "in theory, in principle, in doctrine" (D&C 88:78).

9. The temple is described as a "place of thanksgiving" (D&C 97:13) and a place of "memorials" (D&C 124:39). It is the proper place to "give thanks unto God in the Spirit for whatsoever blessing ye are blessed with" (D&C 46:32). It is the place where "I may reveal mine ordinances," the Lord says (D&C 124:40). In revealing His ordinances, the Lord is revealing things "which have been kept hid from before the foundation of the world" (D&C 124:41). "If thou shalt ask, thou shalt receive revelation upon revelation, knowledge upon knowledge, that thou mayest know the mysteries and peaceable things—that which bringeth joy, that which bringeth life eternal" (D&C 42:61).

10. Finally, the temple is a place of the unifying of all ordinances through firsthand participation. "Reading the experience of others," Joseph Smith said, " . . . can never give *us* a comprehensive view of our condition and true relation to God. Knowledge of these things can only be obtained by *experience*

through the ordinances of God set forth for that purpose."[24] Experience is always more than abstract or conceptual understanding. Through it we can have the very law and power of God written into our flesh, into our "inward parts," our very limbs and tissues. Jesus promised anciently, and again in modern revelation (D&C 88:67), that if our eyes are single to His glory our whole bodies shall be filled with light. (An ancient tradition says that there was a time when the whole body could think. We are promised a time to come when the righteous shall comprehend all things [see D&C 88:67].) The Prophet Joseph summarized the process: "Being born again, comes by the Spirit of God through ordinances."[25] Soul-consuming rebirth comes through the higher ordinances of the temple, which are the reenactment and the dramatic rehearsal of all ordinances of the kingdom of God.

We think, or tend to think, of these as stages through which we pass once and "once and for all." Clearly it is intended that the pattern and order of the house of God is repetitive. There is need for continual participation. Prophets teach that we are only beginning, that we now have only the sign and shadow, as it were, of an eternal order to be opened to us more fully hereafter. "The order of the house of God," the Prophet Joseph said, "has been, and ever will be, the same, even after Christ comes; and after the termination of the thousand years it will be the same; and we shall finally enter into the celestial kingdom of God, and enjoy it forever." Our present temple experiences are "a prelude of those joys that God will pour out on that day" when we inherit the fulness.[26] Our history, like our doctrine, is full of testimony that a temple sacrificially built and faithfully dedicated will bring down the Lord's glory. "My glory shall rest upon it" (D&C 97:15).

When the question is raised, "Why be married in the temple? Why not just elope?" we often say, "Because only temple marriages are forever." But that puts all the emphasis on extent and duration. It says nothing of the quality and power and intensity of the love which can alone justify such duration. So let us rather say: "Because only in the temple are you placed in covenant-harmony with divine powers which will eventually so infuse and fuse your love that it will be worth perpetuating forever."

Sometimes this idea is challenged: "You mean I cannot love my wife or my husband or children fully without some conferral in the temple?"

Our answer: "Exactly."

"You mean that what I am now feeling isn't love?"

"It is the beginning of real love. But a marriage will not last forever based on what you feel now. You must both receive and give an ever richer quality of love. The keys and glory of that love are in the sanctuary where Jesus Christ is present from beginning to end. You cannot begin or continue with each other except with Him."

DEDICATED HOMES

President Harold B. Lee once asked, "If a couple is not yet prepared to be married in the temple, where should they be married?"

His hearers guessed: in the local chapel? in a sequestered cultural hall? in a hall of justice?

"No," Elder Lee replied, "in the home. Next to the temple, the home is the most sacred place on earth."[27]

This insight also quickened the first generation of Saints. After cleaning and ordering their homes, even their hovels, they held a dedicatory service. It was like a fresh beginning, consecrating dwelling and family to holy purposes and cleansing the dwelling of the lingering influences of earlier, perhaps desecrating, inhabitants. With faith and confidence they invoked the priesthood. Patriarchal and matriarchal rights of the parents were embodied in a dedicatory prayer. The act was also a symbol of consecration of ownership now transferred, in spirit at least, to the Lord. The Prophet Joseph Smith himself gathered his family together and went through this process in their modest log cabin in Nauvoo.[28]

Couples in the temple are often counseled that their homes are to become mini-temples. "Even if you have to live in a tent in a vacant lot," President Spencer W. Kimball said, "look upon your home as a sanctuary."[29] (One couple I know remove their shoes before entering their own room.) And the Lord's description of the temple at Kirtland may be applied point for point to the home: "a house of prayer, a house of fasting, a house of faith, a house of learning, a house of glory, a house of order, a house of God" (D&C 88:119), and also a house of worship (D&C 109:14).

But how can this be, we may respond, when a home is a place of hard, manual, sweaty work; a place of fun and hilarity; and a place whereby "all things pertaining to an inferior kingdom" (D&C 130:9) are dumped into our midst via a counterfeit Urim and Thummim called television? Yet the home *can* be all these things. It can surround all of life. "All things unto me are spiritual," the Lord said (D&C 29:34). But the home is, and remains, a sanctuary only to the degree that the persons within it are consecrated. Then, for all of the mixture of laughter and tears, struggle, conflict, and growing pains, there is a tangible difference. People who enter such a home are constrained to acknowledge that it is a place where the Lord's Spirit is recognizable. And all who come, family as well as strangers, are heartened in that atmosphere. We observe that spirit emanating from single-parent homes, too.

Whether parents go through formal dedicatory ceremonies or not, that Spirit should follow our visits to the temple and our expansions of understanding in the gospel that they evoke. The Millennium will come, Elder George Q. Cannon once observed, only when such homes dot the landscape.[30] Eventually they will constitute a far-flung community, a world neighborhood that by its very existence removes the curse of blight and leavens the human family with peace.

President Hugh B. Brown summed it up: "Celestial marriage enables worthy parents to perform a transcendently beautiful and vital service *as priest and priestess in the temple of the home.* This training will help to prepare them for the exalted position of king and queen in the world to come, where they may reign over their posterity in an ever-expanding kingdom."[31]

MAN AND WOMAN AS REDEEMERS

A contemporary writer has observed: "For love to be fulfilling to woman, she must be able to look upon her lover as a redeemer, that is, as an individual who, in the role of God, transforms her in order to make ultimate fulfillment possible for her. . . . This is impossible," the author concludes, "or at best rare."[32]

Recognizing that the statement falls short of the gospel vision, what could make it possible?

1. The man and the woman must have inherited or received supernatural gifts. Otherwise, talk of assuming the "role of God" is terrible presumption.

2. In giving and receiving, both man and woman must be acting in a way that authoritatively represents the Divine. They

would need to be equipped with divine authority, with the holy priesthood.

3. Their relationship to each other could not be just linear but must be triangular. They could reach each other only if they both were centered in God. That would require a covenant, a new covenant, an everlasting covenant, made with God first and then with each other. And that double fidelity—a fidelity to God and to each other—if violated, would mean a withdrawal of transforming power.

4. A union "in the imitation of God"[33] could be achieved only if the ultimate truth about God is that He is perfected in priesthood and parenthood, as the essence of godhood, and that creation and procreation are not mere mortal projections of a fallen world. Instead eternal life is the union of eternal lives. Salvation in marriage is never individual but always dual. President Hugh B. Brown said, "Marriage is and should be a sacrament,"[34] the highest sacrament, the supreme fulfillment of saintliness.

Our temples make possible for us all four of these conditions.

Over the years we have gathered statements, under the label "to the righteous but unmarried," from all of the modern prophets, beginning with Joseph Smith. They uniformly promise that "no good thing" will be withheld from those who are without companions. They counsel against letting discouragement or impatience lead to compromise or a "settle for less" submission to an unbelieving wife or husband. "All in due time." "All in due time."

8

JOSEPH SMITH AND THE KIRTLAND TEMPLE

How early in the Prophet's consciousness did the idea germinate that God would require the building and dedicating of temples and would reveal his ordinances to be performed in them? One way of reading our history is that the first and last revelations in the Doctrine and Covenants that Joseph received concerned the temple, though at first he may not have fully understood this. When the promise about priesthood that is part of section 2 of the Doctrine and Covenants[1] began to be fulfilled through John the Baptist's conferral of priesthood authority, Joseph Smith and Oliver Cowdery were told, "and this shall never be taken again from the earth until the sons of Levi do offer again an offering unto the Lord in righteousness."[2] Oliver Cowdery's wording of that statement is "that the Sons of Levi may yet offer an offering unto the Lord in righteousness."[3] The Prophet later came to understand that this offering relates to the temple.[4]

Elijah is a character whose life and promises apparently were reviewed when Moroni taught the Prophet over successive years. The passages about Elijah in the book of Malachi were quoted to the Prophet at least four times in two successive days in 1823. Somehow the hearts of the fathers would turn to the children and the hearts of the children to the fathers. And this was a key or power which Elijah would reconfer.

Kirtland became the preparatory location for the full restoration of those keys and ordinances. It was a revelatory moment when the Prophet was told that a house must be built, the exact dimensions were spelled out,[5] and he was told that it must be built by the sacrifice of the people—meaning, among other things, that it would not be easy—and that great blessings depended upon the completion of that work. The Church at the time was feeble, struggling, impoverished.

Since the Prophet and the other New York Saints had come to Kirtland, divisions and misunderstandings had developed. A meeting Joseph attended was influenced by the "peepings and mutterings" of false spirits. Philo Dibble recalled that Joseph said, "God has sent me here, and the devil must leave here, or I will."[6] After counsel and ministration, there came a reunion of faith and understanding, and the Saints were given a revelation on how to discern between the Spirit of the Lord and other spirits.

The core questions the Prophet asked then and later regarding spiritual discernment are still applicable today: "Is there any intelligence communicated?" Just babbling or speaking in an unknown tongue is not a communication of truth. Only when it is interpreted by a proper spirit is it so. So the first question was, "Is there any intelligence communicated?"[7] The other question: Is there anything indecorous in the experience? The bouncing, the violent movements, and the hysteria that sometimes attended what people thought were "religious experiences" were condemned by the Prophet as not of God. God's Spirit is a refining and glorifying spirit, not a demeaning one.[8]

The Prophet had begun to establish the orders and patterns of Church organization, as he had been taught them, when the commandment came to build a temple. Financially the people were in severe straits. Sickness was not uncommon. Just to obtain the basic means of survival was difficult for most of the Saints. Nevertheless, soon "great preparations were making to commence a house of the Lord."[9] But in early June 1833 another revelation came in which the Saints were told, "Ye have sinned against me a very grievous sin, in that ye have not considered the great commandment in all things, that I have given unto you concerning the building of mine house" (D&C 95:3).

What was the "very grievous sin"? Apparently it consisted in not considering in all its aspects the commandment to build a temple, a failure to keep the commandments that were designed to prepare the Saints for a great spiritual endowment. What would solve this problem and bring about the endowment "with power from on high"? "It is my will," said the Lord, "that you should build a house. If you keep my commandments you shall have power to build it" (D&C 95:11). Less than two months later, on July 23, 1833, the cornerstones of the Kirtland Temple were laid.

It is instructive to observe here the Lord's warning as to the results of *not* keeping his commandments, words we may take as of general application: "If you keep not my commandments, the love of the Father shall not continue with you, therefore you shall walk in darkness" (D&C 95:12). Note that in this passage *love* seems to be a synonym for *light,* and darkness follows the absence of love. It seems to me that the scriptures show such a close kinship if not identity between light and love in the divine equation that it is impossible to have the one without the other.[10]

Of the building of the Kirtland Temple, Elder Boyd K. Packer has written: "The temple committee and others were soon busily occupied in obtaining stone, brick, lumber and other materials; funds were solicited; labor was donated for the construction; and the sisters provided food and clothes for the workers. The cost of the temple is estimated at $200,000, a very large sum in those days."[11] Several of our historians, Wilford Woodruff included, felt that though the Nauvoo Temple cost much more, it did not require the same level of sacrificial effort. The Kirtland Temple was an unprecedented sacrifice, and it was met with an unprecedented divine outpouring.

The Saints already had many active enemies in the Kirtland area, and when those enemies learned of the intent to build a temple they vowed that it would never be finished—they would see to that! Hence, as the work progressed, enemies made attempts to prevent it. George A. Smith records that for every one man working, the brethren sometimes had three men guarding, some of them armed with pistols.[12] Nevertheless, the work went forward. The Prophet himself, not a skilled workman, could contribute at least his energy and muscle. Wearing his old smock he went into the stone quarry and with his bare hands helped to quarry the stone. By careful organization it was arranged that each seventh day, in this case every Saturday, every wagon the Saints had in the Kirtland area was summoned to haul stone to the temple site. Artemus Millett, a convert from Canada, supervised the construction. Truman O. Angell was the brilliant and inspired architect.[13] He planned and organized every element of the building.

As to the preparatory events, just to lay the cornerstones under crisis conditions was a major problem. Twenty-four Melchizedek Priesthood holders were required for the purpose, and at the time there apparently were not that many in the Kirtland area. Accordingly a few young men of fifteen and sixteen had their ordinations to the higher priesthood hastened, as they were made elders specifically for the purpose. A few older men, somewhat infirm, served as officers in the ceremonies.[14]

The Lord's house is a house of order, and the Prophet Joseph Smith had received a revelation even as to the order of laying cornerstones. Years later, at the laying of the cornerstones of the Manti Temple, Brigham Young arranged (he said this was according to instruction) that the first stone be laid at the southeast corner, the point of greatest light, and at high noon, the time of day when there is the most sunlight.[15] All that is to remind us, we would assume, that the temple is indeed a house of light where the heavenly and the earthly combine.[16]

Several people who lived in Kirtland during the temple-building period have left us their accounts. One was Mary Elizabeth Rollins Lightner, then a young convert. She and her mother were living in Kirtland, and when she discovered the whereabouts of one of the rare copies of the Book of Mormon in that city, she went to the home of Brother Morley and asked to borrow it. He agreed, and she read it so avidly that he let her retain it for that purpose. About the time she finished reading it, the Prophet visited her home and, seeing the book on the shelf, recognized it as the one he had given to Brother Morley. He was most impressed by young Mary, gave her a blessing, and told her to keep the book—he would give Brother Morley another copy.[17]

Mary and her mother went a few evenings later to the Smith home, where others were already assembled. Soon Joseph came in and they held a meeting, the people mostly sitting on boards put across chairs. The Prophet began addressing the group, but after a while he stopped speaking and remained silent. His countenance changed, and it became so white that it seemed transparent. He stood looking intently over the congregation. Finally he spoke. "Do you know who has been in your midst tonight?" Someone said, "An angel of the Lord." And Martin Harris said, "I know— it was our Lord and Savior, Jesus Christ." The Prophet put his hand on Martin's head and said, "Martin, God revealed that to you. Brothers and sisters, the Savior has been in your midst tonight. I want you all to remember it. There is a veil over your eyes, for you could not endure to look upon Him."

Then they knelt in prayer, which he led. His prayer was so long, Mary records, that several people rose and rested and then knelt back down to endure to the end. "Such a prayer," she said, "I have never heard before or since. I felt he was talking to the Lord, and the power rested upon us all."[18]

Later the Prophet gave a blessing to this dear sister. She became one of the faithful who in her ninety-plus years of life endured incredible trials for the faith.[19]

I recount the above story about one of many prayer meetings—John Murdock records several, Eliza R. Snow still others[20]—to show that the outpouring of the Spirit which sometimes attended the Prophet's words was but a foretaste of what was to come through the sacrificial building of the temple.

We have also the testimony of Zera Pulsipher, who was a convert to the Church at this time. He said that when old Father Smith came into the temple (presumably this would have been after its completion, but perhaps it also was before), he looked just like an angel.[21] The venerable, aged father of the Prophet, seasoned and mellowed through much affliction, was a man who commanded the respect of the Saints. The Prophet often put him in charge of fast meetings, and in those days they held them quite often on Thursdays, people putting away their implements, leaving their work where it was and gathering in the spirit of fasting for testimony meetings. In such meetings prayers were often offered, both in private and in public, for the completion of the temple. And one of Father Smith's frequent petitions was that it would be fulfilled upon that temple as on the Day of Pentecost; that is, that the Spirit of God would descend upon it as a rushing, mighty wind, accompanied by tongues of fire. In due time that prayer was answered.[22]

Another witness to this period was a man named Daniel Tyler. He understood from the earliest Kirtland days that the priesthood, which was bestowed to give authority to ordinances, had several branches and ramifications; that the patriarchal priesthood ultimately was the most inclusive and important priesthood, and could be conferred only in a sacred place; that exaltation, as clarified in subsequent revelations, could be received only by priesthood holders and their wives together, and was in effect the extending, magnifying, and intensifying of the patriarchal priesthood throughout the expanding of eternal lives; and that God Himself is the sovereign patriarch.[23]

Hints of that understanding came at Kirtland, but not until Nauvoo did the full scope of the patriarchal priesthood, the temple, and temple marriage become common knowledge to the Saints.[24]

We turn to a brief outline of the actual dedicatory services. Naturally, everyone who had done anything to help with the temple would want to be there at the dedication; and many others who might have been slow to embrace the doctrine or critical or distant would still, out of curiosity, want to be present. The actual capacity of the room is variously estimated. One count of those who came that morning is more than 930 people.[25]

The Prophet had said that if children would be orderly and

were willing to sit on their parents' laps, they could come. That suggestion caught on. It is reported that in the opening session there were two persons in each seat.[26]

The Prophet had held meetings to prepare the Saints, and especially the priesthood brethren, for what was to come. He told them that they must come in purity, having studied and pondered prayerfully the revelations given on the subject.[27] In section 88 of the Doctrine and Covenants the Lord said the temple was to be a house of glory, a house of order, a house of prayer, a house of fasting, a house of God. Some specific commandments accompany those general ones (see D&C 88).

First, those coming into the temple were to be solemn, they were to cast away all light-mindedness. Light-mindedness, in the dictionary sense, is a lack of seriousness, and in the present context can include such attitudes as lack of interest in, making light of, betrayal of, flippant or frivolous approach to, even a ridiculing of, sacred things. Nowhere in the scriptures is lightheartedness condemned, nor again does scripture anywhere forbid a genuine, gentle humor that shows an appreciation for the foibles of ourselves and others. But light-mindedness clearly is inappropriate for Latter-day Saints, especially in the temple setting. In spite of the admonition, however, some found themselves upset, thinking "some mischief was going on."[28] The Saints had been warned: be solemn, avoid light-mindedness.

Second, a series of commandments in section 88 warned the Saints to come purified as far as possible, to sanctify their hearts and hands, to cleanse their lives, to be clean in preparation for bearing the vessels of the Lord (D&C 88:74, 123–26; see also D&C 38:42; 133:5).[29]

Third came an admonition to study—in effect, to read the revelations and to ponder and pray over them. On one occasion, as the climactic promise, the Prophet said to the brethren, "Brethren, all who are prepared, and are sufficiently pure to abide the presence of the Savior, will see Him in the solemn assembly."[30] What a promise!

So between nine hundred and a thousand people assembled early in the morning of March 27, 1836,[31] the Prophet and other authorities of the Church on the stand, and the dedication services began. The Saints had begun gathering at about 7:00 A.M. Joseph the Prophet presided and Sidney Rigdon conducted. President Rigdon first read two of the Psalms—the ninety-sixth and the twenty-fourth. Then the choir sang a hymn written by Parley P. Pratt called "E'er Long the Veil Will Rend in Twain." President Rigdon offered an opening prayer. The congregation then sang a William W. Phelps hymn called "O Happy Souls Who Pray."

President Rigdon then gave a sermon based on Matthew 8:20, where the Master says: "The foxes have holes, and the birds of the air have nests; but the Son of man hath not where to lay his head." He expanded on that theme and gave it a modern interpretation: Anciently the house of the Lord in Jerusalem had been left desolate, the priesthood had become apostate, and Jesus himself had had to drive out of the temple the money changers, abusers, and blasphemers, saying: "It is written, My house shall be called the house of prayer; but ye have made it a den of thieves" (Matthew 21:13). But now, following the dedication, the Kirtland Temple would be the house of the Lord.[32]

The address was appropriate and memorable, and President Rigdon spoke at length. There followed the sustaining of Joseph Smith as prophet and seer, and then the hymn "Now Let Us Rejoice." That ended the morning service.[33]

A brief intermission followed, twenty minutes, long enough

for a few of the sisters to take care of their children. But hardly anyone left. The proceedings then resumed with a hymn, a short talk by the Prophet, and the sustaining of Church leaders in more detailed fashion than is normally employed today. When another hymn had been sung, the moment arrived for which the congregation had waited.

The Prophet arose and gave the dedicatory prayer, a prayer which has been the pattern for all subsequent dedicatory prayers for temples down to the present. That prayer, which now constitutes section 109 of the Doctrine and Covenants, was given to the Prophet by direct revelation. That was a puzzlement to some of the Saints. Strange that God, to whom we pray, should give a revelation telling the Prophet what to pray! But so crucial was that prayer, and so important, that it was given word for word through revelation.

And it is magnificent! Students of Hebrew who know little of Latter-day Saints and less of temples comment that this prayer seems to partake of the Hebraic dualism, the balancing of phraseology and the insights of ancient Israel, that it has echoes and kinship with the prayer fragments we have in the Old Testament relating to the temple of Solomon. And so it does. That is to be accounted for on the ground that the ultimate source of temple worship is not man but God.

"O hear, O hear, O hear us, O Lord," the prayer finished, "that we may mingle our voices with those bright, shining seraphs around thy throne" (D&C 109:78–79).

With the prayer completed, the choir sang that magnificent hymn by William W. Phelps, "The Spirit of God." The dedicatory prayer was accepted by vote, and the sacrament was administered. Then came testimonies from the Prophet, Don Carlos Smith,

Oliver Cowdery, Frederick G. Williams, David Whitmer, and Hyrum Smith.

Finally came the thrice-repeated Hosanna Shout—the first time, so far as I know, that it was used in this dispensation. The Prophet taught them how to do it, and they did it, "sealing it each time with amen, amen, and amen."[34] A shout! Does God want us to shout?

The hymn, written with the light of understanding, says, "We'll sing and we'll shout with the armies of heaven, Hosanna, hosanna to God and the Lamb." Meaning what? Anciently, crying "Hosanna!" with palm branches raised up was actually a two-way reaching. On the one hand it was a plea: "O, save us"—a plea for redemption. On the other hand—as it was in the hearts of those who welcomed Jesus triumphantly into Jerusalem—it was a plea that he enter, that he come; it was an invitation that Christ accept and visit this holy house.[35] To put it in still another way, out of the depths of their souls the congregation expressed their need for Christ, and from the same depths they prayed for him to come. That was done in a shout with the raising of their arms in prayer.

Eliza R. Snow records a remarkable detail. One mother had been turned away at the door because her child was so small, only six weeks old. No one felt that he could endure through the entire day. But Father Smith welcomed the woman and said, "You come, and I promise you all will be well." Psychologists today tell us that children have two instinctive fears (all others they learn): one, the fear of loud noises; the other, the fear of falling. But when this mother rose to join in the Hosanna Shout, the six-week-old child pushed back his coverlet and joined in the shout.[36]

Immediately after the hosannas the Spirit of the Lord descended upon Brigham Young and he spoke in tongues, while another Apostle, David W. Patten, arose and gave the interpretation, then himself gave a short exhortation in tongues. Although there exists hardly a note about the content, these messages were, in essence, words of admonition and of divine approval. The Prophet then arose and left his personal blessing on the congregation, and the service ended at just a little past 4:00 P.M.[37]

What occurred in Kirtland following the dedication was something like a jubilee. The fact that every Saint who could had participated in the dedication either in person or in secondhand awareness drew the Church together into oneness. So intense was that feeling for some days and even weeks that many present thought the Millennium had come, that all tribulation and temptation were past. Such peace was in their hearts that they had no will to do evil. None of the standard battlements were in their lives.

The Prophet had to warn them more than once that all they were experiencing was of God but that, soon enough, opposite experiences would come—the struggles with the adversary and with darkness would be renewed—and that they would know again all the trials that are at the core of saintliness. This was difficult for them to believe.[38] They went from house to house, for example—men, women, children—and would meet together, almost as we do on a beautiful Christmas morning, and would share their impressions, their experiences, each one having his own to report. And often the visitors would say, "I have a blessing for you, Brother," and would bless the other. And the person receiving would say, "I now have a blessing for you," and he would bless the visitor.[39]

Outside the temple, there were both Church members and nonmembers who sensed that something sacred was happening. Even little children did. For example, Prescindia Huntington recalled: "On one occasion I saw angels clothed in white walking upon the temple. It was during one of our monthly fast meetings, when the saints were in the temple worshipping. A little girl came to my door and in wonder called me out, exclaiming, 'The meeting is on the top of the meeting house!' I went to the door, and there I saw on the temple angels clothed in white covering the roof from end to end. They seemed to be walking to and fro; they appeared and disappeared. The third time they appeared and disappeared before I realized that they were not mortal men. Each time in a moment they vanished, and their reappearance was the same. This was in broad daylight, in the afternoon. A number of the children in Kirtland saw the same." When her fellow Saints returned from the temple that evening and reported that during the meeting someone had said that "the angels were resting down upon the house," Prescindia understood.[40]

Some said there was a light—some used the word fire—that emanated from that building, and that at night it still seemed to be illumined. Others, even nonmembers, feeling this outpouring of Spirit, this Pentecost, were caught up in the waves of love and light.[41] It seemed an almost bitter contrast that Joseph should have to say to the Twelve in one of their meetings: "God will feel after you, and He will take hold of you and wrench your very heart strings, and if you cannot stand it you will not be fit for an inheritance in the Celestial Kingdom of God."[42]

How prophetic! Nine of the original Twelve became embittered in varying degrees by that wrenching that eventually came. But in the meantime, and before that darkness, there was more light.

The journals of many who were living in Kirtland at the time describe their activities in this period. They record things such as this: A time or two the Prophet would ask them to come, after fasting, and meet late in the day in the temple, and then would say, "We're going to be here in worship all night." He would instruct them as to the proper order for the meeting, and appropriate prayers would be offered. And then he would tell them to pray silently and then rise and speak as they were impressed by the Spirit.[43] Some spoke prophetically and in tongues, some rose to say they had heard heavenly music, and others rose and said, "I, too, heard it." These were celestial choirs, literally.[44] And there was the remarkable meeting in which a man and a woman arose spontaneously on the impression of the Spirit, sang in beautiful harmony, in language they did not understand, a "song of Zion," beginning and ending each verse together, and then sat down.[45]

We would do well to ponder the harmony of soul that is presupposed in such an experience. Perhaps that is one way in which the promise of the Lord could be fulfilled that we shall one day "see as we are seen and know as we are known" (D&C 76:94; 84:98).

Records of that day speak of remaining in meeting through the night, no one tiring, no one falling asleep, feasting on what the Prophet called the fat things of the Spirit. The effect produced by these meetings was, for many of the Saints, overwhelmingly faith-promoting. But there were some who, instead of being lifted and inspired, felt that somehow this kind of thing was not what was to be expected—as if they had expected either more or less than this.[46] Shortly after these developments, some left the Church.

During the dedication service, angels were seen. Elder Heber C. Kimball testified that "an angel appeared and sat near . . . Joseph Smith, Sen., and Frederick G. Williams, so that they had a fair view of his person." In the evening meeting that day, "the beloved disciple John was seen in our midst by the Prophet

Joseph, Oliver Cowdery, and others."[47] The Apostle Peter also was named.[48]

Eliza R. Snow, herself something of a master of language, wrote: "No mortal language can describe the heavenly manifestations of that memorable day. Angels appeared to some, while a sense of divine presence was realized by all present, and each heart was filled with joy inexpressible and full of glory."[49]

In fulfillment of a promise by Joseph Smith, George A. Smith arose in the evening meeting and began to prophesy. "A noise was heard like the sound of a rushing, mighty wind, which filled the Temple, and all the congregation simultaneously arose, being moved upon by an invisible power; many began to speak in tongues and prophesy; others saw glorious visions." Joseph recorded: "I beheld the Temple was filled with angels."[50]

Oliver B. Huntington later recalled: "Father Smith started up and spoke aloud, 'What's that—is the house on fire?' Some one answered by asking, 'Did not you pray, Father Smith, that the Spirit of God might fill the house as on the day of Pentecost?'"[51]

Now a word about the aftermath. Among the programs established in the midst of the Saints was what was known as the Kirtland Safety Society—a bank which, ironically, turned out to be unsafe. Thwarted by an unexpected refusal of a state charter, its leaders reorganized the society as a joint stock company that would issue notes. Like many other banks of the time, it probably had inadequate reserves *in specie* (most of its assets being in land holdings), so that when redemption of its notes was sought in increasing quantities it was obliged to shut off payments in coin. In the meantime, a spirit of speculation developed and spread rapidly across the nation, and in the financial crisis that ensued when the bubble burst, hundreds of banks were closed.

It has been said that no part of man's anatomy is more

sensitive than his pocketbook. The speculative spirit had become rampant among the Kirtland Saints, and many of them saw this time as their opportunity—perhaps even their blessing—to become wealthy. They took risks, they made foolish decisions. Holding notes from the Kirtland bank, some were bereft of all their meager savings when it failed. Many were terribly bitter as a result. Wrongly, they placed the blame upon the head of Joseph Smith. They failed to separate his roles as a man and as a prophet and to realize that from the start there had been no prophetic promise of success, much less a guarantee.

Seeing the bank's downward course, the Prophet had withdrawn from its leadership early in the summer of 1837. Actually the bank's failure brought him greater economic loss than anyone else. Not only had he bought more shares than any other investor except one, but also, apparently in an effort to prevent the bank from failing, he sold property in Kirtland and also obtained three loans.[52]

The trial that came, as had been prophesied, had its effect in purging the Church of some who had been fair-weather members, and it purged many of the faithful of their more greedy and selfish impulses.

For many years, scholars critical of the Mormon historical past assumed that, since the stock ledger of the Kirtland bank was not available, it had contained a record of illicit transactions. That ledger finally was discovered among documents of the Chicago Historical Society. A comment on this in an article in *BYU Studies* reads: "There are a few irregularities in the ledger, but they do not suggest dishonesty. . . . We now see that the existence of the ledger disproves the allegations of fraud or dishonesty on the part of the Church leaders in Kirtland who had allegedly destroyed the ledger to hide the evidence of their evil."[53]

It is difficult to determine at this point whether it would have been possible in the case of the Kirtland bank to avert the effects of the financial crisis. There is evidence that non-LDS enemies of the Church initiated the run on the bank that caused the suspension of redemption in coin.[54] And Truman O. Angell was convinced that "this institution would have been a financial success and a blessing to the Saints—which they needed very much—had the Gentiles who borrowed the money of the Bank fulfilled their promises."[55]

Later history of the Kirtland Temple was tied up with the changing history of the area. Most of the faithful Saints responded to the call to move to Missouri in 1838–39, but some remained. Another large group moved to Illinois in 1843 to join with the Saints there, leaving a small branch in Kirtland. A few years later apostates took over the temple, and for thirty years or so it was used for both religious and community purposes. Having been abandoned at some stage, it was subjected not only to negligence and the dilapidation produced by time but also to vandalism and destructive pilfering. There is a suggestion, too (though written evidence is scanty), of further pollution of that holy house by its sometime use as a shelter for livestock, stores of hay and straw being piled in the pulpit area where the Lord himself had appeared in that glorious era of dedication and endowment.

In 1880 the Reorganized Church of Jesus Christ of Latter Day Saints (now called the Community of Christ) gained possession of the building. That organization, which subsequently restored the building to its original condition, retains ownership today.[56]

We have left until last the culminating, transcendent events that took place in the Kirtland Temple. At an afternoon meeting there on April 3, 1836, one week following the dedication, the Twelve blessed and the First Presidency distributed the sacrament.

In the reverent spirit thus induced, the curtains that secluded the pulpits from the congregation were lowered and in the pulpit area Joseph Smith and Oliver Cowdery knelt "in solemn and silent prayer."[57] After rising from prayer, they received the glorious visitation first of the Lord Jesus Christ, then of three other heavenly beings.

What then occurred was one of the highest moments in the life of the Prophet Joseph Smith. The veil was taken from their minds, the record says, and they saw the Lord standing upon the breastwork of the pulpit before them. Not exactly on it, for under his feet, says the record, was a paved work of pure gold (D&C 110:1–3). One wonders: could it be that the resurrected, glorified Christ will not again touch directly this inferior planet until he descends upon the Mount of Olives, touches that mount with his celestial foot, and thus sets in train the transformation and the earthquake that prepare the earth for the Millennium?[58] Perhaps so.

The Prophet recorded that the Savior's eyes were as a flame of fire and that his countenance shone above the brightness of the sun. His hair was white as the pure snow, and his voice was as the sound of the rushing of great waters, even the voice of Jehovah. And what did he say? He said who he was. "I am the first and the last; I am he who liveth, I am he who was slain; I am your advocate with the Father" (D&C 110:4). And then came the phrase that must have meant more to Joseph and Oliver than any phrase up until that day: "Behold, your sins are forgiven you; you are clean before me; therefore, lift up your heads and rejoice." They did. "All who are prepared, and are sufficiently pure to abide the presence of the Savior, will see Him in the solemn assembly."[59] They had been declared sufficiently pure.

Then came that series of statements accepting the temple by

Christ himself. "Behold, I have accepted this house, and my name shall be here; and I will manifest myself to my people in mercy in this house. . . . And this is the beginning of the blessing which shall be poured out upon the heads of my people. Even so. Amen" (D&C 110:7, 10).

With that promise made, the Lord having prepared the way for those who were bringing keys from former dispensations, Joseph and Oliver as joint witnesses saw Moses. He conferred upon them the keys of the gathering of Israel and the restoration of the Ten Tribes. Then they saw Elias, who came with what is recorded as the dispensation of the gospel of Abraham, promising both Joseph and Oliver that through them all subsequent generations should be blessed: the same promise that had been made to Abraham thousands of years before (D&C 110:11–12). And then, to crown it all, Elijah came—declaring that the time of Malachi's prophecy about hearts of fathers and children turning to each other had arrived, and conferring the keys of the sealing power. And with all that came the warning—and the promise—that was at the core of the Prophet's first visit from the angel Moroni: "By this ye may know"—now that this has happened, now that Malachi's prophecy is literally fulfilled—"ye may know that the coming of the Lord is nigh, even at the very doors" (D&C 110:13–16).

These visitations constitute the most sublime expression of the entire Kirtland period.

9

ANCIENT TEMPLES AND THE RESTORATION

In an unpublished manuscript titled "Sacred Space in the Fourth Gospel," W. D. Davies wrote: "For many Jews in the first century, as ever since, Yahweh, Israel, and the land—a land which finds its quintessence in Jerusalem and the temple—were joined together by what has been called an unbreakable umbilical cord. This meant that for many religious Jews, the Land Jerusalem and the Temple were of central if not essential importance." Elsewhere Davies shows the duplication of these ideas in "an American key" in Mormonism.[1]

The history of the Latter-day Saints is indeed a history of temples. That history recapitulates much Judeo-Christian experience. Joseph Smith established temples with faith that he was reestablishing them preparatory to the eventual building of temples in both the old and the new Jerusalems. He did not teach that this was a luxurious importation on the restored gospel. It was its center and capstone "to usher in . . . a whole and complete and perfect union, and welding together of dispensations" (D&C 128:18).

Repeatedly the Restoration assumes "the ancient order,"[2] "the order pertaining to the Ancient of Days,"[3] and the "ancient order of things."[4]

The earliest documents of the Restoration movement are replete with references to consecrated land, to Zion, and to "the Lord's house." For converts these became an instant and urgent priority. Even before adequate meeting places or chapels were established, temple land was dedicated at Kirtland, Ohio, in 1833 (D&C 94, 95) and at Adam-ondi-Ahman and Far West, Missouri, in 1838 (D&C 115:7–16). In each case exile followed. In Kirtland, Ohio, in 1836 a "preparatory temple" was completed. From meager resources and with little understanding of the whys, Latter-day Saints of multiple religious and ethnic backgrounds undertook the task amidst severe opposition. ("O Lord, . . . thou knowest that we have done this work through great tribulation" [D&C 109:4–5].) They often labored like Nehemiah with a trowel in one hand and a sword in the other (see Nehemiah 4:16–18). Great dedication is in the record—theirs and that of the temple. But it was soon desecrated and the people dispersed. Within a decade it happened all over again at Nauvoo, Illinois. After only six weeks of ceremonial use, the magnificent Nauvoo Temple was reduced to rubble by arson, and the people were dispossessed of homes and land. The trauma in the loss of two spiritual lodestones—comparable to the double tragedy in Jewish history when the First and Second Temples were desecrated and destroyed—did not diminish the vision. Soon after the vanguard company of pioneers arrived in the Great Basin, Brigham Young pushed his cane into the alkaline soil and said, "Here we will build the temple of our God."[5]

The Latter-day Temple As Center

The centrality of the temple in the Mormon ethos can be seen in other ways.

Latter-day Saints are characterized as city builders and colonizers, as founders. Their communities are seen as a "near-nation" amidst nations. But for Joseph Smith no city or nation was truly a stronghold of Zion that was not crowned by a temple.

Latter-day Saints are characterized as mission-minded on a worldwide scale. Yet Joseph Smith said in 1841 that "labor on the Temple would be as acceptable to the Lord as preaching in the world."[6]

Latter-day Saints are committed to the truism that "a man is saved no faster than he gets knowledge."[7] "The glory of God is intelligence" (D&C 93:36). The university in Nauvoo remained an embryo while the temple was completed. For Joseph Smith there were modes of light and truth—necessary instruction—which could be manifest only by participation in ordinances in a sacred place (D&C 97:13). These, he said, were "things spiritual, and to be received only by the spiritual minded."[8]

Latter-day Saints are recognized as highly organized in a church structure that is elaborate and closely knit. Yet twelve years after its establishment Joseph Smith would say, "The Church is not fully organized, in its proper order, and cannot be, until the Temple is completed, where places will be provided for the administration of the ordinances of the Priesthood."[9]

Latter-day Saints are known for their insistence on "first principles and ordinances" in response to the Atonement of Christ: faith and repentance leading to water baptism and the laying on of hands for the gift of the Holy Ghost. But for Joseph Smith these are first steps toward "those last and more impressive ordinances" of the temple.[10] All offices and ordinations in the priesthood, even the highest, are preliminary to "that which was lost unto you or which he hath taken away, even the fullness of the priesthood" (D&C 124:28). The fullness of the priesthood is received only by the faithful in the house of the Lord. "If a man gets a fullness of the priesthood of God, he has to get it in the same way that Jesus Christ obtained it, and that was by keeping all the commandments and obeying all the ordinances of the house of the Lord."[11]

Latter-day Saints are recognized as a people of consecrated joy, even defiant rejoicing and ceremonial feasting, who "offer up their sacraments" (see D&C 59:9) in the manner of the ancient feasts and who live in hope of the prophetic vision of the eventual messianic banquet. For Joseph Smith the fulness of joy is associated with "the temple of the most high God." Temple dedications were "an event of the greatest importance to the church and the world in making the saints in Zion to rejoice, and the hypocrite and sinner to tremble."[12]

Latter-day Saints are known for coping with crisis—for "taking care of their own." How, then, could they build temples which were a steady drain of treasure and labor? (Joseph said of the temple blessings, "The rich can only get them in the Temple, the poor may get them on the mountain top as did Moses."[13]) The admonition of the Lord was, "Let the Temple be built by the tithing of my people."[14] And so it was. "Neither planting, sowing, or reaping" was permitted to interfere.[15] It is clear that tithing—doubled in labor—was a sacrifice for all. But it was disabling to none. The economic consequences, some immediate, were beneficial. "Some say it is better to give to the poor than build the Temple. The building of the Temple has sustained the poor who were driven from Missouri, and kept them from starving; and it has been the best means for this object which could be devised."[16]

"It shall not impoverish any man but enrich thousands,"[17] said the Prophet.

In sum, Joseph Smith affirmed, "We need the temple more than anything else."[18]

A Prerequisite to Salvation?

In Judaism, Catholicism, and Protestantism one may pose an ultimate question—is any rite, let alone any temple rite, a prerequisite of or instrumental to salvation? For all three traditions the contemporary answer is, in the last analysis, "no."

Orthodox Judaism, since Talmudic days, teaches that "the righteous of all nations will have a share in the world to come." More recently this has been interpreted to mean the righteous of all religions.[19] It follows that many—Gentile as well as Jew—may be granted redemption while totally ignorant of the laws and rites binding upon the observant Jew. This includes the orthodox hope of an eventual renewed temple cultus.

Roman Catholic and Eastern traditions, for all their sacerdotal emphasis, affirm that many who have never sought the holy sacraments may nevertheless receive salvific grace. In certain circumstances, for example, they are assumed to be "baptized by desire." Ronald Knox once summarized the Catholic universal vision by expressing the hope that "many a non-Catholic will show up in heaven with an R. C. [Roman Catholic] tag."[20] Salvation, in short, will not require sacramental channels.

For Protestantism, the doctrine of *sola fide* eliminates the need for any outward signs or works, even those of water baptism or the Lord's Supper. Faith in Christ is sufficient and all-sufficient for salvation. And all "works," including sacerdotal works, are "dead" or, at most, an outward sign.

This is not, of course, to say that these religious traditions abandon ritual. There have been ebbs and flows and liturgical revivals, the invocation of experimental additions and subtractions, embellishments and reductions. The twentieth century witnessed extensive analyses of the functions of ritual—functions which since the Enlightenment are thought to be detached from anything final or fixed. Their justification is construed in terms of historical, social, psychological, symbolic, and existential accounts.[21]

ETERNAL SANCTIONS

Joseph Smith taught that for the ordinances of the temple there were eternal sanctions. These were instituted, set, prepared "before the foundation of the world." This is not to say that there is a Platonic archetype or pure form of the temple that transcends all earthly particulars. It is instead to say, with many strands of Jewish and Christian expectation, that the earthly and heavenly are counterparts.

The Restoration posits an "order of the House of God,"[22] a premortal order introduced repeatedly in the world and now "renewed and confirmed" (D&C 84:48). Men do not here begin in the goodness of God. They continue in it (see D&C 86:11). They are not born into the kingdom of God, but reborn into it (see John 3:5). "Being born again, comes by the Spirit of God through ordinances,"[23] which are essential and exceptionless. Ordinances *confirm* faith in God and His Anointed One; they also enliven it. They signalize the flow of divine grace as one responds to the divine. They also transmit and intensify it "grace for grace." Joseph Smith called these the "power of godliness" (D&C 84:20).

In its patterns of worship, therefore, the temple is, from beginning to end, Christological. Explicit and implicit in everything that is said in Mormon sacred texts is that this temple allegiance is rooted in the New Testament era itself. But outside of Mormonism the New Testament interpretation is dominated by the view that holy places, the temple most of all, are replaced by the Person of Jesus Christ. The most extreme form of this view denies any "geographic theology" and insists that, whatever "sentimental attachment" remained in Paul to the "Temple built with hands," Jesus was and remains the "only true Temple."[24]

Let us briefly outline New Testament evidence that both Jesus and the temple are "true."

JESUS AND THE TEMPLE

Jesus "taught daily in the temple" (Luke 19:47). He spoke of the temple as "my house" (Matthew 21:13) and as "my Father's house" (John 2:16). Literally and symbolically He cleansed it (see Luke 19:45). Some scholars interpret these incidents as Jesus' act of making the temple His own, others as symbols of repudiation.[25] He was condemned because He spoke of destroying and rebuilding "this temple"—but He was speaking of the temple of His own body. Of the Herodian temple, He said, "There shall not be left one stone upon another" (Mark 13:2; Matthew 24:2; Luke 21:6). That can be read as the foreshadowing of the negation of a defunct system, or as an affirmation of the renewed temple—the rebuilding, stone on stone, of the house that was left unto them "desolate" (Luke 13:35).

It is sometimes said that the temple cultus belongs not to Judaism, certainly not to rabbinic Judaism, but to a more primitive period. It can be allegorized. But as Louis Jacobs writes, "The idea of a rebuilt Temple in which animal sacrifices are offered [does not] seem to us the highest to which our religion can aspire."[26]

But what did Jesus really have to do with the ritual system of temple?

Scholars have observed, especially in connection with the Fourth Gospel, that participation in all of the patterns of the temple cultus are demonstrated in Jesus' life and especially in the final week of His life. On His last visit Jesus gave directions for the offering of the Passover lamb.[27] It has even been urged that the Jewish lunar year-cycle, with its temple feasts, sacrifices, and ceremonies, is reflected in perfect sequence in the Gospel of John from chapters 13 to 20.

It is written that Jesus wept over Jerusalem. "O Jerusalem, Jerusalem, . . . how often would I have gathered thy children together, as a hen doth gather her brood under her wings, and ye would not!" (Luke 13:34.) Why *gather*? Joseph Smith's reply:

"It was the design of the councils of heaven before the world was, that the principles and laws of the priesthood should be predicated upon the gathering of the people in every age of the world. Jesus did everything to gather the people, and they would not be gathered. . . .

"The main object [of gathering] was to build unto the Lord a house whereby He could reveal unto His people the ordinances of His house and the glories of His kingdom, and teach the people the way of salvation; for there are certain ordinances and principles that, when they are taught and practiced, must be done in a place or house built for that purpose."[28]

In the Gospel of John we read that in an upper room Jesus said to Peter that the acceptance of the ceremonial washing of feet was essential. Peter's refusal would mean that "thou hast no part [elsewhere translated *inheritance*] with me" (John 13:8). That is strong language. Joseph Smith's translation of the Bible notes that this washing "was the custom of the Jews under their law;

wherefore, Jesus did this that the law might be fulfilled" (JST, John 13:10). Some scholars see this as a custom that Jesus replaced. In the Restoration, the washing of feet is both a preface to and an echo of sacred temple rites, a proper prologue to Jesus' high priestly prayer in John 17 (which is a prayer for unity of Master and disciple as well as of disciple and disciple), and an example of subservience by a true and suffering servant. But it is more. It was given that they might "be clean every whit,"[29] a condition which apparently neither their faith nor their baptism had thus far fully achieved.

The Restoration movement universalizes temple ordinances. All "hard cases" are included—not by exceptionalizing the instruments of God's grace but by revitalizing them, rooting them in the authorities who hold the keys. Temple ordinances are and will be available both on this side and the other side of the veil to all the family of man who have ever lived or ever will live. Thus the acts and Atonement of Jesus Christ may reach consciously and voluntarily to all mankind. "This doctrine appears glorious, inasmuch as it exhibits the greatness of divine compassion and benevolence in the extent of the plan of human salvation."[30]

What is said here of washing applies likewise to ritual ablutions, anointings, covenant makings, and sealings.[31]

ANOINTING

In the epistles of John there is reference to an anointing the faithful have received that "teacheth you of all things" (1 John 2:27). The writer pleads with them to remember this anointing, which "is truth." In the earliest manuscripts the Greek word for this anointing is unique; it occurs nowhere else in the New Testament. It connotes an unguent or "smearing," or, figuratively, an endowment of the Holy Spirit or a consecration to a religious service. Some scholars suggest that it refers to a ritual use of oil. But it has often been read to mean "to appoint" or "to elevate."[32] By either reading, here is a ritual act among Christians—among the Johannine community—that is distinct from baptism and that for the writer of the epistle involves a communion or connection with God that teaches or assures. Its meanings are summed up by the admonition to "abide in him [Christ]."[33] (Compare D&C 88:1–5; 124:124.) In the Restoration this is distinct from the "anointing . . . with oil" spoken of by James, which is for the healing of the sick (James 4:14–15).

THE DOCTRINAL MATRIX

Undergirding all this is what might be called an axiom of continuity between the mortal and immortal spheres. This axiom includes five doctrinal assumptions that are foreign to the philosophical garnishing of both Jewish and Christian thought after the third century: (1) The divine realm is everlastingly involved in space and time. Both are to be sacralized. (2) The world of spirits is near and (though in subtle ways) tangible, not a remnant of superstition or a metaphor. (3) Freedom and the capacity for receiving a full measure of God's truth, way, and life do not end at death. (4) "The elements are the tabernacle of God" (D&C 93:35). "The spirit and the body [together] are the soul of man" (D&C 88:15). Earthly sacramental acts aim at the transformation of the flesh as well as of the spirit. And finally, (5) "In my Father's house are many mansions" (John 14:2); here as hereafter there are many kingdoms and levels of spiritual attainment. When one asks, "Will all mankind be saved?" the question should properly include the corollary, "To what degree?"

TO THE HEBREWS

After the destruction of the temple in A.D. 70, many Jews anticipated a heavenly city and a heavenly temple that would appear on earth more magnificent than any of its predecessors. Some Dead Sea Scroll fragments record the same hope.[34] It was to be erected by divine decree and intervention. Some aspects of Midrashic and rabbinic thought teach that this temple will somehow be "brought" from heaven.

The undergirding theme of the book of Hebrews is that Jesus Christ, by His life and Atonement, renews priesthood, law, ritual, and covenant. The temple may be still standing when He returns. But if the only temple now available is in heaven, then Christ is, in fact, according to Hebrews, offering sacrifice there. The book draws exact parallels between earthly and heavenly temples. Levitical priests, it says, functioned in the earthly sanctuary. Now Jesus, the great High Priest, ministers in the heavenly temple.[35]

With a reverence for the older temple cultus—its meanings, sacrifices, covenants, and functions—the book of Hebrews teaches of Messiah, the Christ, who fulfills temple traditions by becoming the perpetual minister of the people through His bloody covenant and through a heavenly temple ministry.

It has been difficult for scholars to reconcile these chapters with the premise of Christ's "once for all" sacrifice (Hebrews 10:10) on earth, and stranger still to think of anything heavenly needing sanctification, cleansing, and sacrifice. But in Hebrews, Jesus is clearly an active and heavenly high priest; the imagery includes the recognition of angels who attend this sacred service.

Christian orthodox theology today speaks of Christ "as very God of very God." The writer of the book of Hebrews—in the manner of the Restoration—holds that Jesus was indeed Son, Firstborn, Son of Man, Messiah, High Priest, and Apostle. But the writer did not impose the creedal suppositions of the third century.

Hebrews stresses further the prominence of the Melchizedek Priesthood. Melchizedek figures in both Jewish and Christian art through the centuries. But as a source of ordination rights (rites) and powers, his role is obscured. The book of Hebrews makes him, as Albright believed, a legitimate king—his very name meaning "my king is righteousness."

Joseph Smith taught, in defiance of biblical scholarship of his day, that the passage "Though he were a Son, yet learned he obedience by the things which he suffered" (Hebrews 5:8) referred to Melchizedek and not to Jesus. But the book goes on to make Jesus the fulfillment, not only of the Melchizedek type, but also of Abraham and of Moses.

SACRIFICE RESTORED

Similarly, Joseph Smith taught that there were higher ordinances, including sacrifice, for which Moses tried in vain to prepare his people.

"These sacrifices, as well as every ordinance belonging to the Priesthood, will, when the Temple of the Lord shall be built, and the sons of Levi be purified, be fully restored and attended to in all their powers, ramifications, and blessings. This ever did and ever will exist when the powers of the Melchizedek Priesthood are sufficiently manifest; else how can the restitution of all things spoken of by the Holy Prophets be brought to pass. It is not to be understood that the law of Moses will be established again with all its rites and variety of ceremonies; this has never been spoken of by the prophets; but those things which existed prior to Moses' day, namely, sacrifice, will be continued."[36]

Elemental Functions

The modern command to build a temple describes it as "a house of prayer, a house of fasting, a house of faith, a house of learning, a house of glory, a house of order, a house of God" (D&C 88:119).

In all these roles or functions it is a house of covenant, and through all these modes it becomes a house of sanctification. "Holiness" is a term derived from the concept of ritual purity. One must be properly prepared thus to participate in official acts in the presentation or representation of divine service. The idea of *makom kadosh* or "holy house" has Old Testament precedent, not only for the building but for the entire covenant community. In the writings of Paul, as of Peter (see 1 Peter 2:4–9), this house is the focal point for priestly entry, for consecration (both temporal and spiritual). The "chief cornerstone" of the temple, as of the service therein, is the Messiah Himself.[37]

The idea of the temple as a house of prayer and fasting has roots in the ancient order of prayer in which God's name prevails (see 1 Kings 8:28–29). The orthodox Jewish prayer quorum or *minyan* is traceable at least as far back as the Babylonian captivity. And the book of Daniel (see 6:10) spoke of his praying toward the temple three times daily, a practice later encouraged by Joseph Smith.[38]

Proxy Baptism for the Dead

Baptism for the dead, so convention has it, was a non-Christian aberration, perhaps with prior connections to Jewish tomb feasts or burial rites. But historically the evidence can be summed up thus: There is no evidence of this practice among non-Christians. And there is some evidence, in addition to the statement in 1 Corinthians 15:29, that proxy baptism for the dead was practiced among and by early Christians. Indeed, in the iconography, in the typology, and in the baptismal instruction of the early church fathers one may discern at least two different sorts of initiation: one through water baptism and the other through certain initiatory oblations and anointings and baptisms for the dead.[39]

PROXY ORDINANCES

That men and women are privileged to "go through" each and all of the patterns and ordinances for and in behalf of their deceased family members and others is unusual in contemporary religious practice. But, again, proxy and representational ideas are not at the periphery of early Jewish and Christian practice; they are at the core. In the ancient temple, the high priest stood in sacred vestments on the most sacred of ground (the Holy of Holies) on the most sacred of days (the Day of Atonement) and spoke the most sacred of words (YAHWEH, abbreviated to the four consonants YHWH, known as the Tetragrammaton). And he did all this representing the whole house of Israel, who stood thus before God as if they were one man. The Holy of Holies registered or recorded their acts, and the act of cleansing the sanctuary through genuine repentance and sacrifice involved the idea of the "merit of the fathers," as it did the idea of atonement. The related New Testament phrase that has become a prime text in the Restoration is the statement in Hebrews that "they [the dead] without us should not be made perfect" (Hebrews 11:40). (The RSV says "apart from us they should not be made perfect.")

As for Christian understanding, the substitutionary or representational or ransom theories of atonement all presuppose one principle: Christ can merit and mediate for us, speak for us, act for us. Obadiah's expression "saviours . . . on mount Zion" (1:21) is, after all, plural. In Christ's image and through His sanctions and keys and authorities, the faithful may act officially for others. "We are commanded to be baptized for our dead, thus fulfilling the words of Obadiah, when speaking of the glory of the latter-day: 'And saviors shall come up on Mount Zion.'"[40]

THE APOCALYPSE (THE REVELATION OF JOHN)

The *locus classicus* of the temple vision tied to future culmination is the Revelation of John. The Messiah—the Lamb of God—comes down from heaven. The dispersed of Israel are gathered. The church is arrayed like a bride for her husband (Revelation 21:2). Celestial and terrestrial are somehow fused. The New Jerusalem becomes the center of a newly created earth as the preface to a new era, a theocratic community. And the Father and the Lamb as well as the faithful become temples.

The Apocalypse lends itself to fanciful and exaggerated readings. But one theme is inescapable: The temple and its liturgy are the apex of man's earthly quest for the heavenly and of the heavenly transformation of the earthly. Indeed, the promises given the seven churches in the Apocalypse, each one beginning "To him that overcometh," are promises that can be superimposed fittingly on the sequences described in traditional and modern temple worship.[41]

THE SEVEN PROMISES

1. The Tree of Life Promise (see Revelation 2:7): Paradise, spoken of in the Apocalypse, may well refer to Genesis 2:9 and the tree of life in the midst of the Garden. Jewish teaching anticipates that the tree of life will reappear in the messianic era. The book of Revelation identifies the tree of life with, or places it in the midst of, the temple. Pseudepigraphical sources teach of the eventual

role of the Levite priests (whom Joseph Smith said will offer anew in the temple an "offering in righteousness" [see D&C 13:1; 84:31; 124:39]): they will officially remove the threatening sword and cherubim and allow the saintly to eat of the tree of life with its variety of fruits.[42]

2. The Crown of Life Promise (see Revelation 2:10): The imagery of royalty—of scepter, of dominion, of crown, of coronation—runs through the entire book of Revelation. Kingship associated with the priestly roles of Israel is presented in a temple context. The opposite of such a crown is "the second death." The seal, or "sealing in one's forehead," scholars see as associated with security, with victory, with culmination. In the Restoration these sealing powers are reserved for the temple.

3. The Hidden Manna and the New Name Promises (see Revelation 2:17): This manna, some biblical scholars conclude, is "from the tree." To partake of or share in it is to be "partakers of the divine nature" (2 Peter 1:4). Many commentators find here sacramental or eucharistic overtones (see John 6). Again the tree of life is transplanted to the temple and with it the nourishment process.

Names in Jewish thought are theophoric, thought to be all but identical with the personality.[43] To "hold" fast to the name of Christ is to take upon oneself the burdens and characteristics of Christ in covenant relationship. Anciently the name of God was spoken only by the high priest annually within the Holy of Holies. Other traditions say that the name of the Messiah was supposed to be engraved on a stone in the temple. Apocalyptical literature speaks of "plants of renown," renowned men who were surnamed as of Israel. Those thus marked or sealed belong to the glorified Messiah, who in the naming process glorifies them.[44]

4. The Rod (elsewhere translated "scepter") and Morning Star Promises (see Revelation 2:26–28): Authority is promised here as

it is received "of my Father," also the "morning star." Here again the Messiah, or king of Israel, bears the scepter of rule, which ultimately draws together all forms of rule. The promise of power to rule is now shared and legitimized by the Father and the Son— the power to shepherd as Christ does, but also to shatter (see verse 27). Here is portrayed the military and political Savior of Israel arising from Jacob as from Judah. He is fully King of Kings and Lord of Lords, and to his faithful ones are promised kingship and lordship in His likeness. One reading of the gift of the morning star (compare 2 Peter 1:19) is that it is the Son of God Himself (see Revelation 22:16).

5. The White Raiment Promise (see Revelation 3:5): For the Revelator, to be acknowledged before the Father in the presence of His angels is to be reclothed. Jewish tradition stressed the priestly shawl, the priestly robes in the temple, and (among the Essenes) white garments, which were a symbol of inner purity. The Book of Life idea is traceable to Daniel. The related passages on books of remembrance are often seen as the list or registry of those of righteous destiny. Such lists on ancient parchments could be immersed in liquid, hence erased. Ritual ablutions completed by clothing in clean clothes characterize early Jewish and Christian practice. But for the Revelator, as for Joseph Smith, the robes of those in the community of the faithful are delivered by the Messiah to His worthy representatives. This is on a day of fulfillment and of spiritual triumph.[45]

6. The Pillar in the Temple Promise (Revelation 3:12): "Him . . . will I make a pillar in the temple of my God, and he shall go no more out." Written on "the pillar" is the name of God and of the City of God and of the New Jerusalem "which comes down from heaven." In Jewish sources it is said that the Levites were entrusted with the "keys" of the temple, with power to overpower

135

or bind both the evil and the good. (Joseph Smith taught that temple ordinances were given "in order that [one] may be prepared and able to overcome all things" and may learn to "prevent imposition" by the forces of darkness and evil.[46]) In one strand of rabbinic thought, God will restore all crowns to mankind that have been withdrawn from them.[47] The "being written on" recalls the promise of Jeremiah (31:33) that "I will put my law in their inward parts" (compare Hebrews 8:10; 10:16). It was proof of citizenship in the heavenly city. The victory of Christ becomes the victory of Christ's sons.

7. The Promise of a Feast, a Messianic Banquet, the Marriage Supper of the Lamb (Revelation 3:20–21): "To him that overcometh will I grant to sit with me in my throne, even as I also overcame, and am set down with my Father in his throne." The promise is not for the lukewarm but for the fully regenerate. To be anointed is to have one's eyes opened "to the glory of the kingdom" and then to become partaker or "to share" thereof. Such promises are not made on faith alone, but to those whose faith has brought them the mark of the prize of the high calling of Christ. He who will rule and reign forever now promises that His own will rule with Him, will be with Him. And one high symbol of that invitation to share power is the promise of a glorious culminating feast enjoyed by the faithful. Those who have come up through affliction, who have not been defiled, who have had their faith and love tested, are "called, and chosen, and faithful" (Revelation 17:14).[48] They are they who have fully embraced and been embraced in the holiness of God in His sanctuary.

CONCLUSION

One might trace in detail the counterparts and implications of these patterns in the sacred texts of the Restoration. The few points outlined here underscore a simple conclusion: Within the Jewish-Christian tradition one may find the doctrinal and ritual core of the ceremonials of modern Mormon temples. Whatever else Latter-day Saint temple worship may seem to simulate, its deepest roots and closest ties are to those traditions. In fact, Mormon understanding of temples may well be closer to normative Judaism and first-century Christianity than Judaism and present-day Christianity are to each other today. The Mormon temple faith is at once biblical, messianic, and millennial.

10

PUTTING ON THE NAMES:
A JEWISH-CHRISTIAN LEGACY

Aristotle observed that "nothing is by nature a name or a noun." That is, words or word-names have no inherent or necessary meaning. Instead they are arbitrarily assigned to objects or persons. For different reasons, it is a standard view today that names, as well as concrete or abstract terms, are no more than a *flatus vocis,* a mere sound.

This tendency to reduce language to whimsical convention without concern for more profound origins may be symptomatic of the secularization of men and even the trivialization of life itself. At any rate, it reflects a diminishing of the religious consciousness that some names were thought anciently to be of divine origin.

In antiquity, several ideas about names recur, among which are the following:

1. In names, especially divine names, is concentrated divine power.

2. Through ritual processes one may gain access to these names and take them upon oneself.[1]

3. These ritual processes are often explicitly temple related.

The tradition that certain temple-centered names have a divine status is present in the inscriptions of Tel Mardikh, which reach back into the third millennium B.C. There are place names in the tablets of Ebla (Upper Syria) that translate "Temple of the Word." These Canaanites apparently divinized the word *ni'm* (Heb. *Ne'um*), meaning "oracle." And they ascribed a divine status to the voice, the name, the oracle, and *the word* of their god or gods associated with their temple.[2]

The proscription against pronouncing the personal name of deity is also ancient.[3] It relates to the third commandment: "Ye shall not swear falsely by the name of Yahweh or God" (Exodus 20:7; Deuteronomy 5:11). This seems to suggest that one use of God's name is in making a covenant. Related is the idea that one may make a serious and solemn vow by using, taking upon oneself, or acting in the name of God. The proper use of the name *YHWH* constitutes a covenant between Israel and her God.[4]

In Egyptian initiation rites one puts off his former nature by discarding his name, after which he receives a new name. Prior to coronation, the candidate is presented to the gods without his own personal name. In order to pass the obstacles, he recites the name of his god and thus is allowed to pass. If the candidate cannot produce the name, the gatekeepers are aggressive and unyielding.[5]

In the temple ritual setting, names are not seen as mere labels. They mark degrees or attributes or roles in one's transformation process. They are symbolic of new births or beginnings. Thus an individual, while retaining his identity, may take on several names as he moves through stages toward the divine. "To possess knowledge of another's name is to hold some power over him, even if it be the high god himself."[6] The Egyptians went further:

"The name is a person's essence." If his name perishes, he himself does not exist.[7] The person was told, "Thy name lives on earth. . . . Thou dost not perish, thou art not destroyed forever and ever!"[8] Hence, it was important that one's name live in memory, because if the "name lives on earth" the person could "live hereafter."[9] The name, it was believed, enabled his body to survive.[10]

THE HEBREW WORD FOR "NAME"

The Hebrew word for "name" is *shem*. *Ha-Shem* is still used sometimes as a "meta-word,"[11] part of a prayer pattern, used to avoid saying the most sacred name. In Judaism the "sh" (which in English looks like a *W*) has often had ritual importance because it forms a picture of a position of prayer—arms raised above the head.[12] Thus one symbolizes the name in prayer whether or not he actually uses it.

Speculation continues on the derivation of the name of the oldest son of Noah, Shem, from whose name the designation of "Semite" for the peoples of the Near East has been derived.[13] ("Sh" and "s," depending upon the "pointing" of the letter,[14] are different sounds but reflect both the Hebrew and the Arabic values.) Abraham and his descendants are, in turn, descendants of Shem. It is at least possible that some scriptural references to the person Shem and the word *name* reflect the idea that whoever bears that name is like the angel of the Lord's presence. Abraham received, glorified, and sanctified this name. He is a blessing, and his seed bless themselves, precisely because the imprint of that name is upon all of them.

It is hard to exaggerate the richness of a single order of consonants in Hebrew and how many meanings may derive from a given root. By examining variations of vowel "pointing" on divine names, analysis of the ancient sources continues to this day.

Among the Jews, other techniques expand it even more: *Gematria* assigns numbers to consonants and then draws conclusions about matching sets.[15] By acronyms words are derived from first letters of other words. In *notarikon,* letters of words are interpreted as abbreviations of whole sentences, and letters are varied or interchanged according to certain systematic rules.[16]

The twenty-two letters of the Hebrew alphabet were early assigned masculine and feminine values. And much is made of the contrast between such couplets as dark and light, right and left, male and female.[17] Today there is renewed discussion of ways in which words not only name but also function, as in the performative roles they play in ritual expression. Such "linguistic acts" (for example, "I baptize you"), especially in ceremonial form, undergird and override very important life changes.[18]

NAMES AS TITLES

In the Psalms, eleven of which were sung on festive days in honor of royalty, there are many composite names—sentence names or titles—such as "the God of Gods," "the Most High God," "Yahweh the Exalted," and "the Most High Yahweh." Some Psalms are "a litany of sacred names,"[19] as is Psalm 145, which introduces new titles in verses 1, 3, 5, 6, and 7. Praise here becomes synonymous with prayer and vice versa. In the Psalms, the most frequent order of praising is first of Yahweh, then of His works, and finally of His name. Frank Cross Jr. sees Psalm 132 as a "royal hymn" with connections to the tabernacle; he sees Psalm 89 as "from an early Temple liturgy."[20] In the context there is a close association between the name and the glory of God (see Psalms 26:8 and 79:7). "The dwelling place of God" means the place where His glory—His name—dwells.

THE NAME AND SOLOMON'S TEMPLE

After the construction of the First Temple of Jerusalem, Solomon either stood or knelt down[21] upon a platform in the sight of the whole congregation, spread out his hands toward the heavens, and offered a dedicatory prayer. Repeatedly Solomon called the temple "the house I have built for your name"[22] (see 2 Chronicles 6:34, 38). Even the foreigner who implored Yahweh was to know "as your people Israel do" that this house "bears your name." The exact Hebrew reads, "that your name has been *called over*"[23] (2 Chronicles 6:33). The temple is "the place where you promised to put your name, so that you may hear [KJV reads "hearken unto"] the prayer your servant offers toward this place" (2 Chronicles 6:20; 1 Kings 8:29).

From then on, prayers were directed to the temple in the belief that God's presence was there as it was in heaven. Covenanters spoke of "seeing God" as an extension of worshipping in the temple (Isaiah 6:1; Psalm 24:3–6; Matthew 5:8).

The Jews, during the period of the Second Temple, faced the dilemma of avoiding the idolatrous practices of placing statues or idols in their sacred structures. For the Jews, the belief that a temple was dedicated to Yahweh, and that His presence was somehow localized therein, confronted the commandment to avoid images or statues. In Deuteronomy, and especially Jeremiah, the name became a substitute, a legitimate replacement, for forbidden images or replications of the Deity. Somehow, it was believed, the name brought the presence of the *kavod* or glory—a tangible and visible presence—within the most sacred place. A cluster of interrelated expectations revolved around this presence: the priestly literature speaks of the light, the aura, the perpetual flame of tabernacle and temple. Thus, the use of the name of Deity in the temple setting helped to reconcile the ideas of divine transcendence and immanence in the setting of the temple, for the name could be present within the temple while the power of God extended everywhere.

NAMES AND SACRIFICE

For Israelites, the highest moment of feast or sacrifice in the sanctuary was to behold the presence of Yahweh, that is, to be presented at the sanctuary (Exodus 34:23; see Deuteronomy 31:11; Isaiah 1:12).[24] When an altar was built to Yahweh and sacrifice and invocation of His name were appropriately made, it was believed He would come and bless the worshipper. As Kaufmann puts it, "The effect of the offering on the divine realm is depicted not in terms of union, but in terms of God's pleasure at man's submission and obedience." An offering is "a token of honor and reverence. . . . The sacrifice is 'acceptable,' 'delightful,' and 'pleasant' to God."[25] This is the substratum assumption behind most temple laws and narratives. Kaufmann concludes, "The custom of calling altars and sanctuaries by theophoric names is attested to in early times."[26]

In the temple setting it is clear that by proper use of the name or names, one does not speak *of* or *about* God. He speaks *to* or *for* or *with* God.[27] Divine names are uniquely hallowed because they are more than descriptions, however lofty. They are invocations. The question is not "What do you call this 'object'?" but "How may I summon or commune with the Divine?"

THE NAME *YAHWEH*

The supreme or transcendent name of God is in the four Hebrew letters *YHWH*, later known as the Tetragrammaton. The letters have obscure origins, pronunciations, and meanings that continue to confound scholars.[28] But they are usually thought to express the eternity of God—that He was, He is, He shall be, or that His presence shall never depart from Israel. Whatever its meanings, this sacred name, in both early and late Jewish thought, was surrounded with safeguards: It could be spoken only on one day a year—Yom Kippur—and in the most sacred place—the Holy of Holies. The high priest spoke it in behalf of the people-community of all Israel. It was in the performance of his most sacred function, the cleansing of the sanctuary. This meant purifying Israel of her sins.

When the *Kohen Gadol* (high priest) went into the temple on the Day of Atonement, he had already undergone elaborate preparations for purification. The experience was considered awesome, even perilous. Imminent danger as well as redemption was at stake. The pronunciation of the name was thought to bring him into direct contact with the divine. Through the power of the name, he was able to experience God as "a consuming fire."[29] If spoken in unpreparedness or without concentration, it was thought, the name could bring dire, even disastrous, results.[30]

One of the oldest passages of the Mishnah says that the high priest at the appointed place and time on the Day of Atonement offered thrice a certain formula containing the name. The congregation answered after him: "Blessed be the name of the glory of his kingdom for ever and ever."[31] Thus the name of the King of Righteousness became, symbolically, the name of His Righteous Kingdom and of its members. After the third recitation, "the priests and the people who stood in the Court at the time when they heard the Name, coming forth from the mouth of the High Priest, bent the knee, prostrated themselves and fell on their faces and said: 'Blessed be the Name of His Glorious Kingdom forever and ever.'"[32] "The climax of the ceremony was the mighty official proclamation of the sacred cultic name of Yahweh."[33]

The Qumran community, a century and a half before the birth of Jesus, considered themselves a righteous remnant plucked from the midst of a corrupt temple culture. They, too, celebrated the Name.[34] Regarding the Second Temple as defiled and looking forward to a future messianic temple, they performed an annual ritual for renewing their covenant with Yahweh. The process involved ritual ablutions, purifying baths, clothing themselves in white, and praising Yahweh.[35]

BEARING THE NAME

During the First and Second Temple periods, receiving the name was a privilege of obedience. It was to be "inscribed" on and inside the person—in the hands (see Isaiah 56) and on the "inward parts" (Jeremiah 31:31–34). It was to permeate the new heart and new spirit of those who had heretofore profaned the name (see Ezekiel 36:21–28). It was also associated with priestly robes. The headdress both of the ordinary priest and of the high priest[36] (see Exodus 28:6) was a cap "made in the same fashion as that of all the priests." Over this was stitched blue or violet embroidery extending from the nape of the neck to the two temples. The forehead had a plate of gold on which was graven in sacred characters the name of God.[37] The name was expected to be inscribed and present in the new temple (see Ezekiel 43:7) and the new city (see Ezekiel 48:35), where it would signify that "The Lord is there." In deed and in prayer the name was to be retained and honored just as the ark contained the covenant and as the temple contained the ark. Ultimately it was to be as everlasting as the covenants accompanying it. Finally, desecration of names brought the penalty of death (see Leviticus 24:16; 1 Kings 21:10). To sanctify the name, one must be willing to submit to martyrdom.

In Jewish practice to this day, a person who recovers from a severe illness is given a new name which, in effect, celebrates his return from near death. Such a name is new to the person because it is assumed the person is himself new, having overcome or been healed from death. Such new names assigned in prayer are chosen from worthy patriarchs (e.g., Abraham, Isaac, and Jacob) and from worthy matriarchs (e.g., Sarah, Rachel, and Leah). Sometimes the names are compounds of the names of God (see Revelation 2:17).

NAMES AND CREATION

The notion that divine names have creative power and the world itself was made by the use of the holy language is present in a Talmudic statement: "Bezalel knew how to combine the letters [of Hebrew] by which the heavens and earth were created" (see Exodus 31:3; 35:31). It is said that this man was filled with the Spirit of God in *wisdom,* in *understanding,* and in *knowledge.* It goes on to say that by knowledge "the depths were broken up," by wisdom the earth was founded, and by understanding the heavens were established.[38]

In fact, Jewish tradition has sometimes elevated the words of the Torah into divine entities. The words of the Pentateuch were first seen as a total tapestry and unity, not one syllable of which was dispensable. Later the words or names were thought to be organic, in some sense vitalized, so that the names were understood as living supermundane beings. (The Zohar says, "Scripture is like a man and has flesh, soul, and spirit.") The next step was not only to regard the Torah as a composite of the names of God but, as a whole, the one great Name of God.[39]

By the speaking of words (i.e., names), God himself acted in creation. His saying words made light, or the heavens, or the world. The Talmud says all creation was completed by ten utterances.[40] Thus, in Jewish tradition, as one praises the name of God he reaches the very ultimate nature of God. As he verbalizes the name, he is calling upon that nature "at which moment all the creation is at our feet, prepared to do our bidding, because all of creation emanates from that nature."

A prescribed order was required in the use of the names. Rabbi Eleazar said in a well-known midrash on Job 28: "The various sections of the Torah were not given in their correct order. For if they had been given in their correct order, anyone who read them would be able to wake the dead and perform miracles."[41] Exodus 34:5 says, "The Lord came down in a cloud and placed himself beside him [Moses] and proclaimed the name of the Lord." One legend says Moses used that name as his instrument in dividing the Red Sea. Traditions dealing with the creation of the world are matched by traditions concerning the re-creation of man.

There is evidence that the Qumran community and other groups, as well as John the Baptist, set great store upon initiation hymns leading to rebirth or the gift of life. They saw this process as the restoration of God's image. To take the name upon oneself was to take the image of God. Later, the *Odes of Solomon,* a Gnostic group of hymns that date to the first or second century, describe baptism as a sign and as a seal of names.[42] It may be that Paul had this in mind in Ephesians 1:13.

THE NAME OF JESUS

In nothing is Jesus more Jewish than in His use and reverence of the "name of the Father." Jesus says, "I am come in my Father's name" (John 10:25). He speaks of "the works that I do in my Father's name" (John 5:43). He prays, "Father, glorify thy name" (John 12:28). He teaches that prayer addressed to the Father should begin, "hallowed be thy name" (Luke 11:2). His high priestly prayer asks the Father to "keep through thine own name those whom thou hast given me" (John 17:11), and says, "I have declared unto them thy name" (John 17:26). But what of Jesus' own name?[43]

At one point Jesus says to His disciples: "Hitherto have ye asked nothing in my name" (John 16:24). Later He says that some will claim in vain to prophesy in His name and thus to cast out devils and in His name to do many wonderful works (Matthew 6:9; 7:22). He asks His disciples to gather "in my name" (Matthew 18:20). Luke describes the disciples' return, saying that even the demons are "subject unto us through thy name" (Luke 10:17). John speaks of those who "believe on his name" (John 1:12; see John 2:23). All this bespeaks a kinship of Messiah and Father in the tradition of the sacral name and name entitlement.

Jesus, in the book of John, as well as in the epistles of John, bears God's name to the point that He can say, "the Father and I are one" (John 10:30). Does this mean their names are one? The specific divine name that is assumed in these passages is a matter of controversy. Perhaps it is the divine name in Exodus 3:14: "I am." But the Masoretic text can be read to mean "I will become what I will become."[44] This is compatible with the view that Yahweh became the messianic figure of the New Testament. But it is incompatible with the philosophical thesis that God is exclusively "being" without the dimension of "becoming."

In the New Testament, the tradition is carried forward that one can be named by God, or be named after God, or "called" by a name that gives a person a specific mission or commission. Associated with the latter idea is the conviction that by wearing or bearing the name, one is placed under God's special protection, as well as His judgment. (Adam named animals and by so doing attained dominion over them[45] [see Genesis 2:19; Psalm 1:26; 8:6].) It would appear that to take or to give a name without divine authority is, in effect, to illegitimately assume or presume divine honor.

BAPTISM INTO THE NAME

Bible scholar William Albright observes: "There are two kinds of formal statements about baptismal status in the New Testament." One mentions "baptism 'in the name of'" and the other 'into the name of' the Messiah. . . . The first formula ('in the name of') may include both faith in Jesus as Messiah, and also the ceremonial action which accepted this profession of faith—i.e., the baptismal rite. 'Into the name of' . . . calls attention to the results" of baptism. "The neophyte baptized into the name of the Messiah thus not only pledges allegiance to Jesus as Messiah," but is also established or born "into fellowship with him"[46] and with the Father in whose name he acts.

Writing one's own name on a temple wall was thought, in Second Temple times, to unite one with the temple deity. "To bear the name" was a sign of citizenship in the sacred city. Revelation 3:12 makes the new name of Jesus as Lord the insignia of victory. For by bearing the name, one shares in the name and character of Jesus (see Philippians 2:9–10). This is comparable to the promise of being "registered" in the Book of Life (Revelation 13:8; 17:8; 20:12; see also Luke 10:20; Hebrews 12:23).

Baptism, as described in Acts 2:38; 8:16; and 1 Corinthians 1:13, 15, requires one to acknowledge (1) knowing the name, (2) accepting the name, and (3) testifying of the name. This is a blessing, a burden, a commission. The name may have been "Messiah" or the title "Son of Man" or both.

THE DISCIPLES' TRANSMITTAL OF THE NAME

Peter heals in the name of Jesus Christ and explains that there is no other name under heaven given among men by which we can be saved (Acts 4:12; see 2 Nephi 31:21). It is also clear that forgiveness by God comes in the name of Christ, which is also somehow the name of God. (Compare the "forgiveness" from God described in Ezekiel 20:8–9.) To refuse to punish would bring contempt from the Gentiles for the name of God and His power.

By the end of the first century, the *Psalms of Solomon,* a pseudepigraphal work, said, "While your name dwells in our midst, we shall find mercy." This is often interpreted as both a lament and a consolation for the destroyed temple.[47] Thereafter, among the Jews divine names were associated with the Ark of the Covenant in the synagogue and among Christians with emerging sacraments and preachments. The Didache at about A.D. 100 has this sentence: "We thank you, Father most holy, for the sake of your holy name which you made to dwell in our hearts."[48]

The close connection between desecrating the name and desecrating the temple is reflected in the Jewish tradition that the correct pronunciation of the name of God was lost when the temple was demolished by the Romans in A.D. 70. Concern for the recovery of this knowledge, viewed as crucial, is reflected in the mystical tradition that was rediscovered about A.D. 300.[49] Then the Kabbalists gave the name the title *Tetragrammaton,* "the word of four letters," or the square name, or more simply, the square.[50] The tradition continued that the name must remain ineffable, that is, unspeakable, except in ritual contexts. A Gnostic echo of this with allusions to the temple is in the second- or third-century *Gospel of Philip:*

"One single name they do not utter in the world, the name

which the Father gave to the Son, which is above all things, which is the name of the Father. For the Son would not become Father except he clothe himself with the name of the Father. This name those who have it know indeed, but they do not speak of it. But those who have it not do not know it."[51]

This passage is close to another in the *Gospel of Philip* that says Christ did all things in a mystery or sacrament. It names five of these. One involved the receiving of a new name with an anointing that rendered the person Christlike.[52]

The *Gospel of Bartholomew,* also from the third century, incorporates a Jewish legend that "Adam and Eve had characters and signs written on their brows, and the names of the Father, Son and Holy Ghost were written" in certain parts of their bodies.[53] In Egypt as well, similar holy insignia were placed on or in ritual garments.[54]

NAME AND DESTINY

The Hebrew *Apocalypse of Enoch* (fifth century A.D.) became a basic document in Jewish Merkabah throne mysticism, which depends heavily on passages in Ezekiel. There are three main notions of names: (1) that sacred names are engraved "with a pen of flame on the throne of glory," (2) that sacred names "fly off (from the throne of glory) like eagles,"[55] and (3) that there is a heavenly curtain "on which are printed all the generations of the world and all their deeds, whether done or to be done, till the last generation."[56] This curtain was seen as a heavenly counterpart of the temple veil, which in the earthly tabernacle and temple divided the holy place from the Holy of Holies. It was a veil that somehow contained "in blueprint" the whole course of human history.[57] In Jewish thinking, this was a condensation of names, a forecast of destiny that is neither a violation of freedom nor a compromise of individual prophecy.[58] Rabbi Akiba summarized the prevailing view: "All [is] foreseen [and] choice [is] granted."[59] A corresponding notion is that heavenly records are kept and guarded by a heavenly scribe. (The idea that names of the faithful may be written in the Book of Life appears at least as early as in Daniel 12:1–4.)[60]

Name Transmission

Medieval Jewish mysticism continued and embellished—in the absence of the temple—ritual processes for receiving and giving divine names.[61] Thus Eleazar of Worms (about A.D. 1200) describes an initiation, which Scholem concludes is "very old," for the transmitting of the name of God from master to pupil.

"The name is transmitted only to the reserved—this word can also be translated as 'the initiate'—who are not prone to anger, who are humble and God-fearing, and carry out the commandments of their Creator. And it is transmitted only over water. Before the master teaches it to his pupil, they must both immerse themselves and bathe in forty measures of flowing water, then put on white garments and fast on the day of instruction. Then both must stand up to their ankles in the water, and the master must say a prayer ending with the words: 'The voice of God is over the waters! Praised be Thou, O Lord, who revealest Thy secret to those who fear Thee, He who knoweth the mysteries.' Then both must turn their eyes toward the water and recite verses from the Psalms, praising God over the waters."[62]

There may be a link between such patterns and Jewish ritual baths practiced in the time of Jesus. These ceremonies required sizable cisterns or pools and abundant water reserves. Remnants of many such cisterns have been uncovered in and near Jerusalem. Numerous baths have been found in the southeast corner of the

Old City dating back to the Second Temple period.[63] Such ritual baths were preparatory to entry into the Temple Mount. One precept of ritual purity required a "bath . . . [with] no less than forty 'seahs' [about 750 liters] of spring water or rainwater."[64] The insistence not only on water but on running water reflects an earlier Qumran preoccupation. It was also embraced by the Hassidic movement for whom, as Buber writes, "immersion in a river or a stream is higher in value than the ordinary ritual bath."[65] In this context it should be recalled that the Jerusalem Temple was built over flowing water. "A river rises from below the temple," writes Richard Clifford, "and flows out to make the earth fertile."[66] Ezekiel prophesied that out from under the future messianic temple water will flow (see Ezekiel 47:1–12; Genesis 2:10–14).

Another Jewish name-ritual in medieval times was titled "Putting On and Fashioning the Mantle of Righteousness." "A piece of pure deerskin parchment" was cut into a sleeveless garment similar to the high priest's ephod. It covered shoulders, chest, and navel and included a "hat connected with the garment." On this garment the names of God were inscribed. After a period of fasting and ritual purification, and at the end of seven days, one went to the water. On receiving certain signs that confirmed his inward purity, the candidate was considered fit to "put on" the venerable name. He proceeded into the water and emerged from it with the name that it was believed assured him "irresistible strength" and authorized him to invoke angels associated with the name thus acquired.[67]

A thoroughgoing attempt to ascribe a number or a name to every human muscle or nerve, as if the name "governs" the organism, permeates many Jewish movements, for example, the writings of Isaac of Luria (sixteenth century). Similar ritual procedures are thought, under certain combinations, to bring the Holy Spirit.

Breathing or blowing the utterance with the face in the proper position is thought to bring about "communion with His great Name."[68]

NAMES AND MAGIC

In warning and protest against abuses and magical expectations arising from the use of names,[69] Maimonides (1135–1204) and other influential Jewish interpreters tried to draw the line between authentic and spurious practices. Nevertheless, Jewish and Christian lore contains many references to occult incantations and to amulets, charms, spells, exorcisms—all related to speculative angelologies and demonologies.[70] Maimonides tended to interpret passages, both biblical and talmudic, in a figurative way and thus denied the existence of either demons or angels. But wonder-working aspirations continued (and continue) to flourish. Martin Buber's *For the Sake of Heaven* is a striking and lamentable account of the efforts of nineteenth-century Jews to effect and even reverse the outcomes of Napoleonic Wars with occult incantations.[71] In contrast to the magician, the sorcerer, and the conjurer, Jewish rabbis sought to understand name rituals for altruistic and not for manipulative purposes. Merely knowing and repeating the names were not sufficient.

The observant Jew, as the dedicated Christian, claimed to employ these names and invoke these powers either in his quest for divine aid or in his attempt to establish a meaningful relationship between "the above and the below," or in his striving to organize and vitalize his own life.

PHYSICAL CORRELATES

In religious as well as in legal practice, most contemporary cultures have abandoned severe punishments by mutilation for blasphemous use of sacred names. Anciently, it was not so. Among Israelites, blasphemy could bring death by stoning.[72] In other cultures, for abuse of the sacred name one could lose his eyes, his nose, his ears, or his tongue. More radical still were those punishments which left a man a eunuch or impotent, and left a woman barren and hardly recognizable as a woman.

Why such extreme, even fatal, consequences? This brief synopsis points to one answer: Both in Jewish and Christian parlance, divine names were and are a matter of life and death—in every physical and spiritual sense. Life is violated in taking or speaking names "in vain." One who thus profanes is acting in self-destruction, striking at the fountain of his own soul, his nature, the vital places of selfhood. In Hebrew lore, the *loci* of these soul powers were the *neshamah* ("breath"), *ruach* (also "breath" or "vital spirit"), and *nefesh* ("soul").[73]

Such abuse of the divine instrument, which is the self, is all the more serious because the *selem* and the *demut* (the "image" and the "likeness")[74] of God reside in every human self: "Be ye holy for I am holy" (*qadosh;* Leviticus 11:44–45). Once one has partaken of the name, he wears it, he manifests it. A figurative identification tag is attached, as it were, to every element of his being (those who truly know him know him by name). The highest spiritual aspiration is that there will one day be full harmony of nature between the One who names, the name, and the named. This is the vision of the temple in Isaiah 56:

> *For thus says the Lord:*
> *As for the eunuchs who keep my Sabbaths*
> *and choose to do what I will—*
> *holding fast to my covenant—*
> *to them I will give a handclasp and a name*
> *within the walls of my house*

that is better than sons and daughters;
I will endow them with an everlasting name
that shall not be cut off.
And the foreigners who adhere to the Lord
to serve him,
who love the name of the Lord,
that they may be his servants—
all who keep the Sabbath without profaning it,
holding fast to my covenant—
these I will bring to my holy mountain
and gladden in my house of prayer.
Their offerings and sacrifices
shall be accepted on my altar,
for my house shall be known
as a house of prayer for all nations.
Thus says my Lord the Lord,
who gathers up the outcasts of Israel:
I will gather others to those already gathered.[75]

NOTES

1. HOUSE OF GLORY

1. Personal recollection of Robert McKay to author.

2. Matthias F. Cowley, *Wilford Woodruff, Fourth President of The Church of Jesus Christ of Latter-day Saints: History of His Life and Labors as Recorded in His Daily Journals* (Salt Lake City: Bookcraft, 1964), 584.

3. Joseph Smith, *Teachings of the Prophet Joseph Smith*, sel. Joseph Fielding Smith (Salt Lake City: Deseret Book, 1976), 91.

4. Ibid., 161.

5. Hyrum L. Andrus and Helen Mae Andrus, comps., *They Knew the Prophet* (Salt Lake City: Deseret Book, 1999), 139.

6. Melvin J. Ballard, "The Inspiration of Temple Work," *Utah Genealogical and Historical Magazine*, October 1932, 147.

7. John A. Widtsoe, *In a Sunlit Land: The Autobiography of John A. Widtsoe* (Salt Lake City: Milton R. Hunter and G. Homer Durham, 1952), 177.

8. See D&C 97, given in 1833, where the promise refers to the yet to be built temple "in Zion" (v. 10); and *Orson Pratt Discourses* (Salt Lake City: N. B. Lundwall, n.d.), 326–27. A more recent summary

statement is David B. Haight, "Temples and Work Therein," *Ensign*, November 1990, 59.

9. See John A. Widtsoe, "Temple Worship," *Utah Genealogical and Historical Magazine*, April 1921, 56.

10. Joseph Smith, *History of The Church of Jesus Christ of Latter-day Saints*, ed. B. H. Roberts, 2d ed. rev., 7 vols. (Salt Lake City: The Church of Jesus Christ of Latter-day Saints, 1932–51), 2:428; Edward W. Tullidge, *The Women of Mormondom* (1877; reprint, Salt Lake City: n.p., 1965), 101.

2. FOUNDATIONS OF TEMPLE WORSHIP

1. Joseph Smith, *Teachings of the Prophet Joseph Smith*, sel. Joseph Fielding Smith (Salt Lake City: Deseret Book, 1976), 162.

2. Parley P. Pratt, *Key to the Science of Theology* (Salt Lake City: Deseret Book, 1965), 167, 101.

3. Ibid., 101.

3. THE TEMPLE AND THE MYSTERIES OF GODLINESS

1. Joseph Smith, *Teachings of the Prophet Joseph Smith*, sel. Joseph Fielding Smith (Salt Lake City: Deseret Book, 1976), 91.

2. John A. Widtsoe, "The Beginnings of Modern Temple Work," *Improvement Era*, October 1927, 1074.

3. Daniel Tyler, "Incidents of Experience," in *Scraps of Biography: Tenth Book of the Faith-Promoting Series* (Salt Lake City: Juvenile Instructor Office, 1883), 32–33.

4. Brigham Young, *Discourses of Brigham Young* (Salt Lake City: Deseret Book, 1946), 345.

5. John Taylor, in *Journal of Discourses*, 26 vols. (London: Latter-day Saints' Book Depot, 1854–86), 24:264.

6. Brigham Young, in *Journal of Discourses,* 26 vols. (London: Latter-day Saints' Book Depot, 1854-86), 11:371–72.

7. Smith, *Teachings of the Prophet Joseph Smith*, 367.

8. Discourse of Brigham Young, 6 April 1845, in Joseph Smith, *History of The Church of Jesus Christ of Latter-day Saints*, ed. B. H.

Roberts, 2d ed. rev., 7 vols. (Salt Lake City: The Church of Jesus Christ of Latter-day Saints, 1932–51), 6:230.

9. Journal History, 4 March 1844, LDS Church History Library, Salt Lake City, Utah.

10. Smith, *History of the Church*, 6:545.

11. Smith, *Teachings of the Prophet Joseph Smith*, 237; see Smith, *History of the Church*, 5:2.

12. Wilford Woodruff, in *Collected Discourses Delivered by President Wilford Woodruff, His Two Counselors, the Twelve Apostles, and Others*, ed. Brian H. Stuy, 5 vols. (Burbank, Calif.: BHS Publishing, 1987–92), 5:188–89.

13. John A. Widtsoe, "Temple Worship," *Utah Genealogical and Historical Magazine*, April 1921, 63.

14. Smith, *Teachings of the Prophet Joseph Smith*, 364.

15. Smith, *History of the Church*, 3:295; see Smith, *Teachings of the Prophet Joseph Smith*, 137.

16. Joseph Smith, *The Words of Joseph Smith: The Contemporary Accounts of the Nauvoo Discourses of the Prophet Joseph Smith*, comp. and ed. Andrew F. Ehat and Lyndon W. Cook (Orem, Utah: Grandin Book, 1991), 418; punctuation added for clarity.

17. Parley P. Pratt, in *Journal of Discourses*, 2:43–47.

18. Smith, *Teachings of the Prophet Joseph Smith*, 324.

19. Ibid., 232.

20. Parley P. Pratt, *Key to the Science of Theology* (Salt Lake City: Deseret Book, 1965), 120–21.

21. N. B. Lundwall, *The Vision, or The Degrees of Glory* (Salt Lake City: Bookcraft, 1951), 141.

22. Wilford Woodruff, in *Utah Genealogical and Historical Magazine*, October 1922, 150.

23. Wilford Woodruff, *The Discourses of Wilford Woodruff, Fourth President of The Church of Jesus Christ of Latter-day Saints*, ed. G. Homer Durham (Salt Lake City: Bookcraft, 1990), 158.

24. St. George Historical Record, 1864–1902, LDS Church History Library, Salt Lake City, Utah.

25. Smith, *Teachings of the Prophet Joseph Smith*, 237.

26. Melvin J. Ballard, "The Inspiration of Temple Work," *Utah Genealogical and Historical Magazine*, October 1932, 147.

27. Smith, *Teachings of the Prophet Joseph Smith*, 307.

4. BLESSINGS OF THE TEMPLE

1. See Shaye J. D. Cohen, "The Temple and the Synagogue," in *The Temple in Antiquity: Ancient Records and Modern Perspectives*, ed. Truman G. Madsen (Provo, Utah: BYU Religious Studies Center, 1981), 151–74.

2. Joseph Smith, *History of The Church of Jesus Christ of Latter-day Saints*, ed. B. H. Roberts, 2d ed. rev., 7 vols. (Salt Lake City: The Church of Jesus Christ of Latter-day Saints, 1932–51), 2:428; D&C 109:36–37.

3. Hugh Nibley, *The Message of the Joseph Smith Papyri: An Egyptian Endowment* (Salt Lake City: Deseret Book, 1975), 154–55.

4. Joseph Smith, *The Words of Joseph Smith: The Contemporary Accounts of the Nauvoo Discourses of the Prophet Joseph Smith*, comp. and ed. Andrew F. Ehat and Lyndon Cook (Orem, Utah: Grandin Book, 1991), 196.

5. HOUSE OF GLORY, HOUSE OF LIGHT, HOUSE OF LOVE

1. Franklin D. Richards, in *Collected Discourses Delivered by President Wilford Woodruff, His Two Counselors, the Twelve Apostles, and Others*, ed. Brian H. Stuy, 5 vols. (Burbank, Calif.: BHS Publishing, 1987–92), 3:234.

2. Brigham Young, in *Journal of Discourses*, 26 vols. (London: Latter-day Saints' Book Depot, 1854–86), 9:33.

3. Abraham Joshua Heschel, *Israel: An Echo of Eternity* (New York: Farrar, Straus & Giroux, 1969), 225.

4. Henry B. Eyring, "That We May Be One," *Ensign*, May 1998, 68; see also Mosiah 3:19.

5. Joseph Smith, *Teachings of the Prophet Joseph Smith*, sel. Joseph Fielding Smith (Salt Lake City: Deseret Book, 1976), 162.

6. Joseph Smith, *The Words of Joseph Smith: The Contemporary Accounts of the Nauvoo Discourses of the Prophet Joseph Smith,* comp. and ed. Andrew F. Ehat and Lyndon W. Cook (Orem, Utah: Grandin Book, 1991), 4.

7. Ibid., 203.

8. Jeffrey R. Holland and Patricia T. Holland, *On Earth As It Is in Heaven* (Salt Lake City: Deseret Book, 1989), 94.

9. John A. Widtsoe, "Temple Worship," *Utah Genealogical and Historical Magazine,* April 1921, 56.

10. James E. Faust, "How Near to the Angels," *Ensign,* May 1998, 97.

11. Smith, *Teachings of the Prophet Joseph Smith,* 51.

12. Boyd K. Packer, "The Holy Temple," *Ensign,* February 1995, 36.

13. Carlos E. Asay, "The Temple Garment: 'An Outward Expression of an Inward Commitment,'" *Ensign,* August 1987, 22.

14. Widtsoe, "Temple Worship," 63.

15. Personal conversation with Truman G. Madsen.

16. Robert L. Millet, *Alive in Christ: The Miracle of Spiritual Rebirth* (Salt Lake City: Deseret Book, 1997), 28.

17. Merlin Myers, "Kinship, Religion, and the Transformation of Society," devotional address, Brigham Young University, Provo, Utah, 1 April 1975, notes in possession of author.

18. Wendy L. Watson, "Change: It's Always a Possibility," devotional address, Brigham Young University, Provo, Utah, 7 April 1998, reprinted at www.speeches.byu.edu.

19. Richards, in *Collected Discourses,* 3:234.

20. Smith, *Teachings of the Prophet Joseph Smith,* 90.

21. Joseph Smith, *History of The Church of Jesus Christ of Latter-day Saints,* ed. B. H. Roberts, 2d ed. rev., 7 vols. (Salt Lake City: The Church of Jesus Christ of Latter-day Saints, 1932–51), 1:133.

22. Smith, *Words of Joseph Smith,* 123.

23. Howard W. Hunter, *The Teachings of Howard W. Hunter,* ed. Clyde J. Williams (Salt Lake City: Bookcraft, 1997), 233.

24. Howard W. Hunter, "A Temple-Motivated People," *Ensign,* February 1995, 2.

25. Mary Finlayson to Ann N. Madsen, 17 April 1995.

26. Smith, *Teachings of the Prophet Joseph Smith*, 326.

27. Ibid., 232.

28. Parley P. Pratt, *Key to the Science of Theology* (Salt Lake City: Deseret Book, 1965), 101.

29. Personal conversation; used by permission.

30. Personal conversation; used by permission.

31. Lorenzo Snow, in Journal of B. H. Roberts (uncataloged), April 1893, 193, Archives of The Church of Jesus Christ of Latter-day Saints.

32. Bruce C. Hafen, "Come, Come Ye Saints," annual university conference, Brigham Young University, Provo, Utah, 28 August 1995, notes in possession of author.

33. Orson Pratt, in *Journal of Discourses*, 16:82.

34. Smith, *Teachings of the Prophet Joseph Smith*, 296.

35. Wilford Woodruff, *Wilford Woodruff's Journal, 1833–1898*, ed. Scott G. Kenney, 9 vols. (Midvale, Utah: Signature Books, 1983–85), 5:135–37; spelling and capitalization standardized.

36. Minutes of Relief Society Organization, Salt Lake City, 1842, Archives of The Church of Jesus Christ of Latter-day Saints.

37. Sheri L. Dew, address in Logan, Utah, March 1998; notes by Mindy Davis.

6. Elijah and the Turning of Hearts

1. Elden J. Watson, *Manuscript History of Brigham Young, 1846–1847* (Salt Lake City: Elden J. Watson, 1971), 540.

2. Ibid., 529.

3. Ibid., February 23, 1847, 529–30.

4. Melvin J. Ballard, in Conference Report, October 1912, 108.

5. Joseph Smith, *Teachings of the Prophet Joseph Smith*, sel. Joseph Fielding Smith (Salt Lake City: Deseret Book, 1938), 159.

6. Ibid., 232.

7. Ibid., 323.

8. Ibid., 321.

9. Joseph Smith, *History of The Church of Jesus Christ of Latter-day*

Saints, ed. B. H. Roberts, 2d ed. rev., 7 vols. (Salt Lake City: The Church of Jesus Christ of Latter-day Saints, 1932–51), 5:23.

10. Robert Frost, "The Death of the Hired Man," in *Robert Frost Poetry and Prose,* ed. Edward Connery Lathem and Lawrance Thompson (New York: Henry Holt and Company, 1984), 21.

11. Smith, *Teachings of the Prophet Joseph Smith,* 330.

12. Ibid.

13. Erastus Snow, "A Journal or Sketch of the Life of Erastus Snow," typescript, BYU Special Collections.

14. "Characteristic Sayings of President Lorenzo Snow," *Improvement Era* 22 (June 1919): 651.

7. PURPOSES OF THE TEMPLE

1. Joseph Smith, *Teachings of the Prophet Joseph Smith*, sel. Joseph Fielding Smith (Salt Lake City: Deseret Book, 1976), 191.

2. John A. Widtsoe, *A Rational Theology As Taught by The Church of Jesus Christ of Latter-day Saints,* 7th ed. (Salt Lake City: Deseret Book, 1965), 127.

3. John A. Widtsoe, "Temple Worship," *Utah Genealogical and Historical Magazine,* April 1921, 62.

4. Harold B. Lee, "When Your Heart Tells You Things Your Mind Does Not Know," *New Era,* February 1971, 3.

5. Joseph Smith, *History of The Church of Jesus Christ of Latter-day Saints,* ed. B. H. Roberts, 2d ed. rev., 7 vols. (Salt Lake City: The Church of Jesus Christ of Latter-day Saints, 1932–51), 5:2.

6. Ibid., 3:380.

7. Hugh Nibley, *Temple and Cosmos: Beyond This Ignorant Present,* ed. Don E. Norton, vol. 12 of *The Collected Works of Hugh Nibley* (Salt Lake City: Deseret Book and FARMS, 1992), 15.

8. George F. Richards, "Temple Service," *Utah Genealogical and Historical Magazine,* October 1928, 149.

9. James E. Talmage, *Jesus the Christ* (Salt Lake City: Deseret Book, 1982), 395 n. 2.

10. Widtsoe, "Temple Worship," 63.

11. Melvin J. Ballard, "The Inspiration of Temple Work," *Utah Genealogical and Historical Magazine*, October 1932, 147.

12. Widtsoe, "Temple Worship," 55.

13. Smith, *Teachings of the Prophet Joseph Smith*, 91.

14. Harold B. Lee, *Youth and the Church* (Salt Lake City: Deseret Book, 1970), 140.

15. Smith, *Teachings of the Prophet Joseph Smith*, 91.

16. Joseph Fielding Smith, "The Pearl of Great Price," *Utah Genealogical and Historical Magazine*, July 1930, 103.

17. Sandra L. Richter, *The Deuteronomistic History and the Name Theology* (Berlin and New York: Walter de Gruyter, 2002), 55.

18. Nephi Jensen, "The Abundant Life," *Improvement Era*, March 1951, 168.

19. Widtsoe, "Temple Worship," 56.

20. Joseph Fielding Smith, "The Los Angeles Temple," *Improvement Era*, November 1951, 798.

21. Smith, *Teachings of the Prophet Joseph Smith*, 323.

22. John A. Widtsoe, *Gospel Interpretations: Aids to Faith in a Modern Day*, (Salt Lake City: Bookcraft, 1947), 103.

23. Smith, *Teachings of the Prophet Joseph Smith*, 274.

24. Ibid., 324.

25. Ibid., 162.

26. Ibid., 91.

27. Harold B. Lee, as recalled by Brent Goates.

28. Spencer W. Kimball, *Faith Precedes the Miracle* (Salt Lake City: Deseret Book, 1972), 262, 264.

29. Spencer W. Kimball, "Counsel on Marriage," Archives of The Church of Jesus Christ of Latter-day Saints.

30. George Q. Cannon, Logan Temple cornerstone ceremony, 19 September 1877; quoted in Nolan Porter Olsen, *Logan Temple: The First 100 Years* (Providence, Utah : K. W. Watkins, 1979), 34.

31. Hugh B. Brown, *You and Your Marriage* (Salt Lake City: Bookcraft, 1960), 193.

32. Peter Koestenbaum, *Religion in the Tradition of the Phenomenology* (Princeton, New Jersey: D. Van Nostrand Co., 1967), 34–35.

33. Hyrum Smith, as quoted in Joseph Fielding Smith, *Life of Joseph F. Smith* (Salt Lake City: Deseret Book, 1938), 114.

34. Brown, *You and Your Marriage*, 13.

8. JOSEPH SMITH AND THE KIRTLAND TEMPLE

1. "Behold, I will reveal unto you the Priesthood, by the hand of Elijah the prophet, before the coming of the great and dreadful day of the Lord" (D&C 2:1). This section contains portions of Moroni's words to the Prophet on the night of September 21, 1823.

2. See D&C 13, given on May 15, 1829. The sons of Levi anciently attended to the temple sacrifice, presumably offering it in unrighteousness during their apostasy. In the last days they shall offer it in righteousness in a restored temple.

3. Joseph Smith–History 1:71, footnote.

4. See D&C 128, where the offering includes the presenting of accurate records. Compare D&C 124:37–39, where "your memorials for your sacrifices by the sons of Levi" are included as part of the order to be performed "in a house which you have built to my name."

5. See D&C 94, given on May 6, 1833. An earlier admonition about the house of the Lord to be built was given on December 27, 1832 (see D&C 88:119). The dimensions were not spelled out until the following May.

6. Philo Dibble, "Recollections of Joseph Smith," *Juvenile Instructor* 27 (January 1, 1892): 23. See historical headnote to D&C 50.

7. Joseph Smith, *Teachings of the Prophet Joseph Smith*, sel. Joseph Fielding Smith (Salt Lake City: Deseret Book, 1976), 204; Joseph Smith, *History of The Church of Jesus Christ of Latter-day Saints*, ed. B. H. Roberts, 2d ed. rev., 7 vols. (Salt Lake City: The Church of Jesus Christ of Latter-day Saints, 1932–51), 4:572. This is from an editorial ascribed to Joseph Smith appearing under the title, "Try the Spirits."

8. Speaking of "fallings, twitchings, swoonings, shaking, and trances," Joseph wrote, "Now God never had any prophets that acted in this way; there was nothing indecorous in the proceeding of the Lord's prophets in any age; neither had the apostles nor prophets in the apostles' day anything of this kind" (Smith, *Teachings of the Prophet*

Joseph Smith, 209). Compare Mother Smith's account of Joseph's comments: "When a man speaks by the Spirit of God, he speaks from the abundance of his heart—his mind is filled with intelligence, and even should he be excited, it does not cause him to do anything ridiculous or unseemly" (Lucy Mack Smith, *History of Joseph Smith by His Mother* [Salt Lake City: Bookcraft, 1979], 194).

9. Smith, *History of the Church,* 1:349.

10. D&C 88:40 teaches that as intelligence cleaves to intelligence, and virtue to virtue, so does light to light. And surely love begets love.

11. Boyd K. Packer, *The Holy Temple* (Salt Lake City: Bookcraft, 1980), 129. For an early reckoning of costs, see *Latter-day Saints' Messenger and Advocate* 1 (July 1835): 147–48; *The Latter Day Saints' Millennial Star* 14 (September 4, 1852): 438; *Contributor* 13 (April 1892): 251.

12. George A. Smith says that "they carried pistols about 3 in. long." Sometimes they were stoned. See also Smith, *History of the Church,* 2:2. "We were obliged to keep up night watches to prevent being mobbed" (Journal of Joel Hills Johnson, entry of September 23, 1835).

13. See Journal of Truman O. Angell, LDS Church History Library, Salt Lake City, Utah.

14. Brigham Young, in *Journal of Discourses,* 26 vols. (London: Latter-day Saints' Book Depot, 1854–86), 1:133–35; Andrew Jenson, *Historical Record* 5:75.

15. Hugh Nibley, *The Message of the Joseph Smith Papyri: An Egyptian Endowment* (Salt Lake City: Deseret Book, 1975), 154.

16. On laying the first cornerstone at the "south-east corner" in harmony with the "strict order of the Priesthood," see Smith, *History of the Church,* 4:331. See also Joseph's use of the phrase, "Jesus Christ being the chief cornerstone," in his letter to Isaac Galland, March 22, 1839, in Joseph Smith, *The Personal Writings of Joseph Smith,* ed. Dean Jessee (Salt Lake City: Deseret Book, 1984), 418.

17. See Mary Elizabeth Rollins Lightner, in "Mary Elizabeth Rollins Lightner," *Utah Genealogical and Historical Magazine* 17 (July 1926): 193–95; Hyrum L. Andrus and Helen Mae Andrus, comps., *They Knew the Prophet* (Salt Lake City: Bookcraft, 1974), 22–23.

18. See *Young Woman's Journal* 16 (December 1905): 556–57; Andrus and Andrus, *They Knew the Prophet*, 23–24.

19. See "The Testimony of Mary Elizabeth Rollins Lightner," April 14, 1905, Brigham Young University Special Collections and Manuscripts, Harold B. Lee Library. These remarks were given when she was eighty-seven years old.

20. See "Records of Early Church Families," *Utah Genealogical and Historical Magazine* 28 (1937): 61; Eliza R. Snow, *Eliza R. Snow, an Immortal: Selected Writings of Eliza R. Snow* (Salt Lake City: Nicholas G. Morgan Sr. Foundation, 1957), 60–64.

21. See Zera Pulsipher papers, Archives of The Church of Jesus Christ of Latter-day Saints.

22. See note 51 herein.

23. See 1878 LDS Church History Library, statement of Daniel Tyler, citing D&C 124, LDS Church History Library, Salt Lake City, Utah; also *Juvenile Instructor* 15 (May 15, 1880): 111–12.

24. See the discourses of Joseph Smith in August 1843, and notes, in Joseph Smith, *Words of Joseph Smith: The Contemporary Accounts of the Nauvoo Discourses of the Prophet Joseph Smith,* comp. and ed. Andrew F. Ehat and Lyndon W. Cook (Orem, Utah: Grandin Book, 1991), 236–48, 300–308.

25. The official history says "probably five or six" hundred "assembled before the doors were opened." An overflow meeting was held in a nearby schoolhouse. Even then "many were left out" (Smith, *History of the Church,* 2:410–11). Later dedicatory services were held to accommodate many others.

26. See Jillaine K. Baker, "The Dedication of the Kirtland Temple," typescript, copy in possession of author.

27. See, for example, the meeting on Thursday, January 14, 1836, where "rules and regulations to be observed in the 'House of the Lord'" were drafted, all to enhance the order, dignity, and worship in the building (Smith, *History of the Church,* 2:368–69).

28. See George A. Smith's comments in *Journal of Discourses,* 2:215.

29. Following such a course of sanctification can prepare us to eventually become the very vessels of the Lord. Section 93, for instance,

teaches that we may "receive a fulness" through worship—a fulness of truth, of light, and of glory (D&C 93:9–20).

30. Smith, *Teachings of the Prophet Joseph Smith*, 92; Smith, *History of the Church*, 2:310.

31. Smith, *History of the Church*, 2:410; compare Archibald F. Bennett, "The Kirtland Temple," *Utah Genealogical and Historical Magazine* 27 (April 1936): 86.

32. Smith, *History of the Church*, 2:413–16.

33. Ibid., 2:416.

34. This shout, Joseph said, "sealed the proceedings of the day" (Smith, *History of the Church*, 2:427).

35. The Saints are commanded to bless the name of the Lord with "loud" voices and "with a sound of rejoicing" by Hosanna—see D&C 19:37; 36:3; 39:19; 124:101. At times in the Kirtland Temple they also used an expression from 3 Nephi: "Blessed be the name of the Most High God!" (3 Nephi 11:17; see also D&C 39:19). Joseph records going home after a night of praise and blessing in the Kirtland Temple, and "my soul cried hosanna to God and the Lamb, through the silent watches of the night" (Smith, *History of the Church*, 2:387).

36. See *Journal History*, October 1909; Snow, *Eliza R. Snow, an Immortal*, 62.

37. The histories make no mention of a benediction either in the morning or the afternoon session. Perhaps the Saints did not consider the meetings closed, since they returned for further meetings. See Baker, "The Dedication of the Kirtland Temple," 14.

38. Daniel Tyler wrote of this period of dedication: "All felt that they had a foretaste of heaven. In fact, there were several weeks in which we were not tempted of the devil; and we wondered whether the millennium had commenced. At or near the close of the endowments, the Prophet Joseph . . . said: 'Brethren, for some time Satan has not had power to tempt you. Some have thought that there would be no more temptation. But the opposite will come; and unless you draw near to the Lord, you will be overcome and apostatize'" (see *Scraps of Biography* [Salt Lake City: Juvenile Instructor Office, 1883], 32–33).

39. Erastus Snow, for one, records: "In the evening they ate the passover and feasted upon bread and wine until they were filled, and

after these things were over the disciples went from house to house breaking bread and eating it with joyful hearts, being filled with the spirit of prophecy; and the sick were healed and Devils were cast out" (Journal of Erastus Snow, 1836, 8).

40. See recollection of Prescindia Huntington in Edward W. Tullidge, *The Women of Mormondom* (New York: Tullidge and Crandall, 1877), 207. Joseph describes an earlier meeting where "the gift of tongues fell upon us in mighty power, angels mingled their voices with ours, while their presence was in our midst, and unceasing praises swelled our bosoms for the space of half an hour" (see entry of January 22, 1836, in diary of Joseph Smith, 1835–36, 141; Smith, *Personal Writings of Joseph Smith,* 148–49).

41. Of the evening of the dedication day, when the Prophet met with the priesthood quorums and another great outpouring of the Spirit took place, it is recorded: "The people of the neighborhood came running together (hearing an unusual sound within, and seeing a bright light like a pillar of fire resting upon the temple) and were astonished at what was taking place. This continued until the meeting closed at 11:00 P.M." (Smith, *History of the Church,* 2:428).

42. This is John Taylor's recollection. See *Journal of Discourses,* 24:197.

43. Smith, *History of the Church,* 2:387–92, 430–33. Jeremiah Willey records: "Joseph Smith requested the Elders to speak their feelings freely and sing, exhort and pray as the Spirit should give utterance. The meeting continued the whole night. Many of the gifts were poured out upon the people; at break of day we were dismissed" (Autobiography of Jeremiah Willey, 10–12).

44. Zina D. Huntington and her sister Prescindia "both heard, from one corner of the room above our heads, a choir of angels singing most beautifully. They were invisible to us, but myriads of angelic voices seemed to be united in singing some song of Zion, and their sweet harmony filled the temple of God" (see Tullidge, *Women of Mormondom,* 207–8).

45. Prescindia Huntington recalled: "Brother McCarter rose and sang a song of Zion in tongues; I arose and sang simultaneously with him the same tune and words, beginning and ending each verse in

perfect unison, without varying a word. It was just as though we had sung it together a thousand times" (as cited in Tullidge, *Women of Mormondom,* 208–9).

46. George A. Smith recalled that some felt "too little" and some "too much" (*Journal of Discourses,* 2:215).

47. As cited in Orson F. Whitney, *Life of Heber C. Kimball* (Salt Lake City: Bookcraft, 1992), 91, 92.

48. "When the afternoon meeting assembled, Joseph, feeling very much elated, arose the first thing and said the personage who had appeared in the morning was the Angel Peter come to accept the dedication" (Journal of Truman O. Angell, 5).

49. Snow, *Eliza R. Snow, an Immortal,* 62.

50. Smith, *History of the Church,* 2:428. The Prophet records the seeing of angels. Others who left records in their journals include Brigham Young, Joel H. Johnson, and Erastus Snow. Among the women who recorded these events were Eliza R. Snow and Prescindia Huntington. See, for example, Brigham Young in S. Dilworth Young, *"Here Is Brigham . . . ": Brigham Young, The Years to 1844* (Salt Lake City: Bookcraft, 1964), 143.

51. *Young Woman's Journal* 8 (February 1897): 240. Joseph and his father had made the same request—the former in the dedicatory prayer (see D&C 109:36–37). Oliver Cowdery wrote under the date of March 27, 1836, which was Sunday, the day of dedication: "In the evening I met with the officers of the church in the Lord's house. The Spirit was poured out—I saw the glory of God, like a great cloud, come down and rest upon the house, and fill the same like a mighty rushing wind." There were 316 present for this meeting (see Leonard J. Arrington, ed., "Oliver Cowdery's Kirtland, Ohio, 'Sketch Book,'" *Brigham Young University Studies* 12 [Summer 1972]: 426).

52. See D. Paul Sampson and Larry T. Wimmer, "The Kirtland Safety Society: The Stock Ledger Book and the Bank Failure," *Brigham Young University Studies* 12 [Summer 1972]: 427–36; Scott H. Partridge, "The Failure of the Kirtland Safety Society," *Brigham Young University Studies* 12 [Summer 1972]: 437–54.

53. Sampson and Wimmer, "The Kirtland Safety Society," 436.

54. Milton R. Backman, *The Heavens Resound: A History of the*

Latter-day Saints in Ohio 1830–1838 (Salt Lake City: Deseret Book, 1983), 318.

55. Journal of Truman O. Angell.

56. Backman, *The Heavens Resound,* 368–72; McGavin, "The Kirtland Temple Defiled," *Improvement Era,* October 1940, 594–95.

57. Smith, *History of the Church,* 2:435; historical headnote to D&C 110.

58. See Proclamation of the Twelve, 1845, in James R. Clark, ed., *Messages of the First Presidency of The Church of Jesus Christ of Latter-day Saints,* 6 vols. (Salt Lake City: Bookcraft, 1965–75), 1:258.

59. Smith, *Teachings of the Prophet Joseph Smith,* 92. Three years earlier Joseph had written the following to W. W. Phelps on January 11, 1833: "We greatly fear before the Lord lest we should fail of this great honor which our Master proposes to confer on us; we are seeking for humility and great faith lest we be ashamed in his presence" (Smith, *Personal Writings of Joseph Smith,* 263).

9. ANCIENT TEMPLES AND THE RESTORATION

1. W. D. Davies, "Israel, the Mormons and the Land," in Truman G. Madsen, ed., *Reflections on Mormonism: Judaeo-Christian Parallels,* Religious Studies Monograph Series, vol. 4 (Provo, Utah: Religious Studies Center, Brigham Young University, 1978), 91.

2. Joseph Smith, *History of The Church of Jesus Christ of Latter-day Saints,* ed. B. H. Roberts, 2d ed. rev., 7 vols. (Salt Lake City: The Church of Jesus Christ of Latter-day Saints, 1932–51), 4:492.

3. Joseph Smith, *Teachings of the Prophet Joseph Smith,* sel. Joseph Fielding Smith (Salt Lake City: Deseret Book, 1976), 237.

4. Ibid., 223.

5. Seymour B. Young, Conference Report, October 1910, 25.

6. Joseph Smith, *The Words of Joseph Smith: The Contemporary Accounts of the Nauvoo Discourses of the Prophet Joseph,* comp. and ed. Andrew F. Ehat and Lyndon W. Cook, Religious Studies Monograph Series (Orem, Utah: Grandin Book, 1980), 6:70.

7. Smith, *Teachings of the Prophet Joseph Smith,* 217.

8. Smith, *History of the Church,* 5:2.

9. Smith, *Teachings of the Prophet Joseph Smith*, 224.

10. Ibid., 362.

11. Smith, *History of the Church*, 5:424.

12. Journal History of The Church of Jesus Christ of Latter-day Saints, January 6, 1842, LDS Church History Library, Salt Lake City, Utah.

13. Smith, *History of the Church*, 4:608.

14. Smith, *Teachings of the Prophet Joseph Smith*, 230; see also D&C 97:10–14.

15. Ibid., 196.

16. Ibid., 329.

17. "A Few Items from a Discourse Delivered by Joseph Smith," July 19, 1840, LDS Church History Library, Salt Lake City, Utah.

18. Journal History, May 4, 1844.

19. C. G. Montefiore and H. Loewe, *A Rabbinic Anthology* (New York: Schocken Books, 1974), xiv.

20. Related to the author by the Jesuit priest Gustave Weigel.

21. See, for example, Abraham Kaplan, "Explanations of Ritual," Presidential Address, Israel Philosophical Association, May 1983.

22. For the Lord's will concerning the order of his house, see D&C 88:119, 127, 128; 128:5, 12; 132:8.

23. Smith, *Teachings of the Prophet Joseph Smith*, 162.

24. C. K. Barrett, *The Gospel According to St. John*, 2d ed. (Louisville, KY: Westminster John Knox Press), 201.

25. Raymond E. Brown, *The Gospel According to John*, Anchor Bible (Garden City, N.Y.: Doubleday and Company, 1970), 172.

26. Louis Jacobs, *A Jewish Theology* (New York: Behrman House, 1973), 300.

27. See "Jewish Background to Christian Worship," in R. J. Beckwith, *The Study of Liturgy* (New York: Oxford University Press, 1978), 42.

28. Smith, *Teachings of the Prophet Joseph Smith*, 308.

29. Ibid., 91.

30. Ibid., 192.

31. In 1835 Joseph Smith spoke of "the order of the house of God," including the ordinance of washing of feet, as "calculated to unite our

hearts, that we may be one in feeling and sentiment, and that our faith may be strong, so that Satan cannot overthrow us, nor have any power over us here" (Smith, *Teachings of the Prophet Joseph Smith*, 91; see D&C 88:138–41).

32. Geza Vermes, *Jesus the Jew: A Historian's Reading of the Gospels* (New York: Macmillan, 1973), 158.

33. Raymond E. Brown, *The Epistles of John*, Anchor Bible (Garden City, N.Y.: Doubleday and Company, 1982), 341–49.

34. R. Williamson, "Platonism in Hebrews," *Scottish Journal of Theology* 16 (1963): 418–19.

35. It was customary for centuries to suppose that "the (one) temple" was the temple in Jerusalem and that Jewish faith made no room for others. But now at Arad a temple has been uncovered known to be contemporary with Solomon's temple. Its design includes an altar and a first tent or curtain, then a second curtain, and a holy of holies (see Y. Aharoni, "Arad: Its Inscriptions and Temple," *Biblical Archaeologist* 31 [1968]: 18–27).

36. Smith, *Teachings of the Prophet Joseph Smith*, 173.

37. See B. Gartner, *The Temple and the Community and the Qumran and the New Testament* (Cambridge, 1965).

38. Smith, *Teachings of the Prophet Joseph Smith*, 161.

39. Roger J. Adams, "The Iconography of Early Christian Initiation: Evidence for Baptism for the Dead" (unpublished ms., 1977); Hugh Nibley, "Baptism for the Dead in Ancient Times," *Improvement Era* 51–52 (Dec. 1948–Apr. 1949): passim; Bernard M. Foschini, "Those Who Are Baptized for the Dead," *Catholic Biblical Quarterly* 13 (1951): 328–44.

40. Smith, *Teachings of the Prophet Joseph Smith*, 223.

41. James E. Talmage, *The House of the Lord: A Study of Holy Sanctuaries, Ancient and Modern*, reprint ed. (Salt Lake City: Bookcraft, 1962); Boyd K. Packer, *The Holy Temple* (Salt Lake City: Bookcraft, 1980).

42. *Testament of Levi* 18:9–12.

43. See Joseph Smith's dedicatory prayer at the Kirtland Temple (D&C 109) and the response, "My name shall be here" (D&C 110:7; compare 1 Kings 8:29).

44. J. Massyngberde Ford, *Revelation* (Garden City, N.Y.: Doubleday and Company, 1975), 400.

45. Joseph Smith's translation of the New Testament parable of the marriage supper notes that those who are "called" but not "chosen" are those who "do not have on the wedding garment" (JST, Matthew 22:14).

46. Smith, *Teachings of the Prophet Joseph Smith*, 91; *Words of Joseph Smith*, 21, n. 21.

47. *Sabbath* 88a, in *The Babylonian Talmud*, trans. Rabbi Dr. I. Epstein (London: Soncino Press, 1938), 1:418.

48. Compare Smith, *Teachings of the Prophet Joseph Smith*, 42.

10. PUTTING ON THE NAMES: A JEWISH-CHRISTIAN LEGACY

1. Dallin H. Oaks, "Taking upon Us the Name of Jesus Christ," *Ensign*, May 1985, 80–83; Numbers 6:27; Mosiah 5:6–12.

2. Mitchell J. Dahood, "The Temple and Other Sacred Places in the Ebla Tablets," in Truman G. Madsen, ed., *The Temple in Antiquity: Ancient Records and Modern Perspectives* (Provo, Utah: Religious Studies Center, Brigham Young University, 1984), 86.

3. E. A. Speiser, *Genesis,* Anchor Bible (Garden City, NY: Doubleday, 1964), 16.

4. Yehezkel Kaufmann, *The Religion of Israel from Its Beginnings to the Babylonian Exile,* trans. Moshe Greenberg (Chicago: University of Chicago, 1960), 298.

5. Hugh Nibley, *The Message of the Joseph Smith Papyri: An Egyptian Endowment* (Salt Lake City: Deseret Book, 1975), 219.

6. Nibley, *Joseph Smith Papyri,* 140.

7. J. Zandee, *Death as an Enemy* (Leiden: Brill, 1960), 14, quoted in Nibley, *Joseph Smith Papyri,* 139.

8. Nibley, *Joseph Smith Papyri,* 139–40.

9. Gertrud Thausing, *Der Auferstehungsgendanke in Ägyptischen Religiosen Texten* (Leipzig: O. Harrassowitz, 1943), 5, quoted in Nibley, *Joseph Smith Papyri,* 139–40.

10. Nibley, *Joseph Smith Papyri,* 140.

11. F. Brown, S. R. Driver, and C. A. Briggs, *A Hebrew and English Lexicon of the Old Testament* (Oxford: Clarendon, 1974), 1028.

12. The prayer posture symbolized by the Hebrew letter for "sh," "shin," may be traced to an Old Testament verse: Abraham replies to the king of Sodom, "I have lift[ed] up mine hand unto the Lord, the most high" (Genesis 14:22). In Hebrew it means literally, "I raised up my hand." It is an oath formula; see Speiser, *Genesis*, 104–5, n. 22.

13. Samuel N. Kramer, *The Sumerians: Their History, Culture and Character* (Chicago: University of Chicago Press, 1963), 298–99. Kramer, an expert on Sumerian, believes that the word *shem* derives from the name *Sumer.*

14. In Hebrew, vowels are designated by dots or points below the consonants, hence the term "pointing." The arrangement and number of dots determine the vowel sound.

15. Gershom Scholem, "Gematria," in *Encyclopedia Judaica*, 16 vols. (Jerusalem: Macmillan/Keter, 1971–72), 7:370–74.

16. See "Notarikon," in *Encyclopaedia Judaica*, 12:1231; Gershom Scholem, *Major Trends in Jewish Mysticism* (New York: Schocken Books, 1946), 99.

17. See Charles Poncé, *Kabbalah* (London: Quest Books, 1973), 249.

18. See John L. Austin's account of "performative utterance," e.g., "I christen you," "I pronounce you man and wife," "I baptize you." In each case saying is a form of doing (see *Philosophical Papers* [Oxford: Oxford University Press, 1979], ch. 10).

19. See Mitchell Dahood, *Psalms,* Anchor Bible, 3 vols. (Garden City, NY: Doubleday, 1970), 3:xxxviii; see 259, 336.

20. See Frank M. Cross Jr., "The Priestly Tabernacle in the Light of Recent Research," in Madsen, *The Temple in Antiquity,* 98–99. See Psalm 132:12–13.

21. Both standing and kneeling are represented on ancient monuments. See Jacob Myers, *II Chronicles,* Anchor Bible, 2 vols. (Garden City, NY: Doubleday, 1965, 1974), 2:36.

22. On building a house to the name of the Lord, see 2 Samuel 7:13; 1 Kings 3:2; 5:3, 5; 6:1–38; 7:13–51; 8:16–18, 20, 29, 43–44; 9:3, 7; 18:32 ("an altar in the name of the Lord"); 2 Kings 21:4;

1 Chronicles 22:7–8, 10, 19; 28:3; 29:16; 2 Chronicles 2:1, 4; 6:5, 7–10, 20, 33–34, 38; 7:16; 20:8–9; Ezra 6:12; Nehemiah 1:9. The people of Israel and the Holy City itself also bear the name.

23. See Jacob Myers, *II Chronicles,* 2:35, n. 33.

24. Richard D. Barnett, "Bringing the God into the Temple," in *Temples and High Places in Biblical Times,* ed. Avraham Biran (Jerusalem: Hebrew Union College, 1981), 10–20.

25. Kaufmann, *The Religion of Israel,* 112.

26. Ibid., 138, n. 3.

27. Louis Jacobs, explaining Buber, in *A Jewish Theology* (New York: Behrman House, 1973), 54. See also his "Excursus: The Name of God," ch. 10.

28. A Palestinian targum identifies the divine name *YHWH* as expressing God's eternal presence with Israel. Robert Hayward has written that this name is at the core of covenant terminology of covenant oaths and was associated with the Jerusalem temple (see *Divine Name and Presence* [Totowa, NJ: Allanheld, Osmun, 1981], 17–20, 82).

29. See *3 Enoch* 42 in James H. Charlesworth, ed., *Old Testament Pseudepigrapha,* 2 vols. (Garden City, NY: Doubleday, 1983), 1:293.

30. Talmudic traditions say that the unpronounceable or secretly pronounced tetragrammaton was trusted only to priests who were pious, chaste, and discreet. When singing from the Torah, the rabbi would "gulp the pronunciation amid the singing of his brethren." Rabbis continue to do so today in "a chant reminiscent of the singing of the Temple priests." See C. G. Montefiore and H. Loewe, *A Rabbinic Anthology* (New York: Schocken Books, 1965), 14.

31. M *Yoma* 3:8; 6:2, citing Leviticus 16:30 in Herbert Danby, tr. and ed., *The Mishnah* (Oxford: Oxford University, 1933), 165, 169; see Hayyim Schauss, *The Jewish Festivals* (New York: Schocken, 1962), 136–38, who gives greater emphasis to the name with his translation. "Blessed be the Name, the glory of His kingdom forever and ever."

32. I. Abrahams, *Studies in Pharisaism and the Gospels,* 2 series in 1 vol. (New York: KTAV, 1967), 2:25.

33. Hans-Joachim Kraus, *Worship in Israel: A Cultic History of the Old Testament,* trans. Geoffrey Buswell (Richmond, VA: John Knox, 1966), 213.

34. Yigael Yadin, ed., *The Temple Scroll,* 3 vols. plus supplement (Jerusalem: Israel Exploration Society, 1977–83), 1:279: "The city which I will hallow by settling my name and [my] temp[le within it] shall be holy and clean." In many Qumran texts the name of God is written in a distinctive script to remind the reader that it is too holy to pronounce. In the Temple Scroll, however, the author, who perhaps thought of his writing as the very law of God, wrote the letters for YHWH in the exact style of the rest of the text; see *The Temple Scroll,* 3:36 (plate 36) for two examples of YHWH in the standard script of the text.

35. J. Massyngberde Ford, *Revelation,* Anchor Bible (Garden City, NY: Doubleday, 1975), 123.

36. Josephus, *Jewish Antiquities* III, 157–58.

37. Josephus, *The Jewish War* V, 235–36. A "crown [with] sacred letters . . . in four vowels," i.e., YHWH. The golden diadem (Exodus 28:36 and 39:70) contained "seal engravings." Hebrew sources claim that the diadem had in it the words "Holiness to Yahweh." The exact rabbinical phrase is *kodesh le-Yahweh.* See TB *Shabbat* 63b. Other sources, including Philo, *De Vita Mosis* II, 114, 132, claim it was simply the tetragrammaton. Gregory of Nyssa, II, 201, describes the gold letters as "ineffable," in Gregory of Nyssa, *The Life of Moses,* trans. Abraham J. Malherbe and Everett Ferguson (New York: Paulist Press, 1978), 106. See Menahem Haran, *Temples and Temple Service in Ancient Israel* (Oxford: Clarendon, 1978), 169. The Holy Name may have been abbreviated (Haran, 34, n. 38) on the headplate (TB *Shabbat* 63b).

38. TB *Berakhot* 55a.

39. Abraham J. Heschel ("The Mystical Element in Judaism," in *The Jews, Their History, Culture, and Religion,* ed. Louis Finkelstein, 3rd ed., 2 vols. [New York: Harper, 1960], 2:943) writes of this approach to the Torah: "The Torah is the 'Holy of Holies'; it consists entirely of the name of the Holy One, blessed be He. Every letter in it is bound up with that Name."

40. See TB *Abot* 5: 1.

41. Gershom Scholem, *On the Kabbalah and Its Symbolism,* trans. Ralph Manheim (New York: Schocken, 1946), 37.

42. See discussions on baptism in the *Odes of Solomon* in

Charlesworth, *The Old Testament Pseudepigrapha,* 2:728 and n. 31, and 732; see also J. H. Bernard, *The Odes of Solomon,* in *Texts and Studies,* 10 vols. (Cambridge: Cambridge University, 1912), 8 (3): 42.

43. A Jewish midrash claims that the name of the Messiah "existed . . . in an incomplete form" before the creation. See Samuel Rapaport, *Genesis Rabba I,* in *A Treasury of the Midrash* (New York: KTAV, 1968), 42.

44. W. F. Albright, "Further Observations on the Name Yahweh and Its Modifications," *Journal of Biblical Literature* 44 (1925): 158–62.

45. Markus Barth, *Ephesians 1–3,* Anchor Bible (Garden City, NY: Doubleday, 1974), 383.

46. William F. Albright and C. S. Mann, *Matthew,* Anchor Bible (Garden City, NY: Doubleday, 1971), 362.

47. Not only destruction but desecration and defilement of the temple led to a loss of the knowledge of names. Ezekiel 8 describes how the temple was entered by idolaters. Images were engraved all around the walls, and the seventy men of the elders of the house of Israel were standing before them. In the inner court of the temple between the porch and the altar, twenty-five men were prostrating themselves east-ward toward the sun. This was, in Greenberg's phrase, the "climactic abomination"—turning one's back to the sanctuary and bowing toward the sun; see Moshe Greenberg, *Ezekiel 1–20,* Anchor Bible (Garden City, NY: Doubleday, 1983), 171; see 164–74.

48. Raymond E. Brown, *The Epistles of John,* Anchor Bible (Garden City, NY: Doubleday, 1982), 711.

49. David Noel Freedman concludes that the pronunciation was lost "some time during the Middle Ages" and efforts were made "in the modern period . . . to recover the pronunciation." See *Theological Dictionary of the Old Testament,* 5:500.

50. Greenberg, *Ezekiel 1–20,* 174–75.

51. *Gospel of Philip* 102:5–13, section 12. The translation and num-bering system are in R. M. Wilson, *The Gospel of Philip* (New York: Harper & Row, 1962), 30; see *The Nag Hammadi Library,* trans. James M. Robinson (San Francisco: Harper and Row, 1977), 133, *Gospel of Philip* 54:5–13, with a translation by Wesley W. Isenberg and an alter-nate numbering system.

52. *Gospel of Philip* 115:27–30, cited as section 68 in Wilson, *The Gospel of Philip,* 43; cited as 67.27–30 in Robinson, *The Nag Hammadi Library,* 140.

53. Nibley, *Joseph Smith Papyri,* 190.

54. Ibid.

55. *3 Enoch* 39:1, in Charlesworth, *Old Testament Pseudepigrapha,* 1:290–91, see 246, 249–52.

56. *3 Enoch* 45:1, in Charlesworth, *Old Testament Pseudepigrapha,* 1:296.

57. *3 Enoch* 45:1–2; Exodus 26:31; 2 Chronicles 3:14.

58. The length of the "garment" in later Kabbalah included two hundred thirty-one "gates" which were, in fact, "possible combinations of the 22 letters of the Hebrew alphabet." Its width was a numerical "elaboration of the Tetragrammaton"; see Gershom Scholem, "Kabbalah, in *Encyclopaedia Judaica,* 10:591.

59. Louis Finkelstein, *Akiba: Scholar, Saint and Martyr* (New York: Covici Friede, 1936), 204.

60. *3 Enoch* 44, in Charlesworth, *Old Testament Pseudepigrapha,* 1:295–96, note 44t. Apocryphal literature, especially Enoch material, eventually links Enoch and Metatron, both of whom write and record the merits or demerits of Israel. In *3 Enoch,* Enoch, now called Metatron, is even called "the lesser Yahweh," *Yahweh ha-Qatan,* thus *3 Enoch* 12:5: "And he called me 'the lesser Yahweh' in the presence of all his heavenly household; as it is written *For my name is in him* (Exodus 23:21)." See John Bowker, *The Targums and Rabbinic Literature* (Cambridge: Cambridge University Press, 1969), 150 and note a; see 144–49.

61. Scholem describes the notion of a "cosmic veil or curtain before the throne which conceals the glory of God from the host of angels." Allowing that the idea is very old, at least as old as the Aggadah of the second century and citing *Pistis Sophia* of the Gnostics, he says, describing a passage in the book of *Enoch,* it "contains the images of all things which since the day of creation have their pre-existing reality, as it were, in the heavenly sphere. All generations and all their lives and actions are woven into this curtain; he who sees it penetrates at the same time into the secret of Messianic redemption, for like the course of history, the

final struggle and the deeds of the Messiah are already pre-existently real and visible." This summarizes his account of Merkabah mysticism. See Scholem, *Major Trends in Jewish Mysticism,* 72; source for the *Pistis Sophia* is from Karl Schmidt's German translation of 1925, 35; the reference for the book of *Enoch* is *3 Enoch* 45, in Charlesworth, *Old Testament Pseudepigrapha,* 1:296–99. In Scholem's discussion of the theory of magic, n. 130 refers to *Midrash Tehillim,* edited by Buber.

Letters and combinations have cosmic power. Scholem says that one of the "related processes to ascending to the throne is 'the putting on, or clothing, of the name,' a highly ceremonious rite in which the magician impregnates himself, as it were, with the great name of God." The Hebrew phrase is *lavosh et-hashem.* There is a Syriac phrase in the *Odes of Solomon* 39:7. He also compares it to Paul's statement in Romans 13:14: "put ye on the Lord Jesus Christ." See Scholem, *On the Kabbalah,* 136, and n. 3. The magician "performs a symbolic act by clothing himself in a garment into whose texture the name has been woven." He claims the rite is described in a manuscript in the British Museum. See Scholem, *Major Trends in Jewish Mysticism,* n. 132; also n. 112 to lecture IV, 77.

62. Scholem, *On the Kabbalah,* 136.

63. Nahman Avigad, *Discovering Jerusalem* (Jerusalem: Shikmona, 1980), 139–43.

64. Avigad, *Discovering Jerusalem,* 139.

65. Martin Buber, *Tales of the Hasidim: The Early Masters*, trans. Olga Marx (New York: Schocken, 1947), 328.

66. Richard J. Clifford, "The Temple and the Holy Mountain," in Madsen, *The Temple in Antiquity,* 122.

67. Scholem, *On the Kabbalah,* 136–37.

68. Ibid., 188.

69. Louis I. Rabinowitz et al., "Maimonides," in *Encyclopaedia Judaica,* 11:754–81.

70. An introduction to the subject of demons both in the Bible and in extracanonical literature is in T. H. Gaster, "Demon, Demonology," in *Interpreter's Dictionary of the Bible,* 4 vols. (New York: Abingdon, 1962), 1:817–24.

71. Martin Buber, *For the Sake of Heaven,* trans. Ludwig Lewisohn (New York: Harper, 1953).

72. Leviticus 24:11–16; see "Blasphemy," in *Encyclopaedia Judaica* 4:1073–74.

73. Brown, Driver, and Briggs, *A Hebrew and English Lexicon of the Old Testament,* 675, 924–26, 659–61, respectively; see Scholem, *On the Kabbalah,* 195–96.

74. Brown, Driver, and Briggs, *A Hebrew and English Lexicon of the Old Testament,* 853–54, 198, respectively.

75. *The Apocalyptic Book of Isaiah: A New Translation with Interpretative Key,* trans. Avraham Gileadi (Provo, Utah: Hebraeus Press, 1982), 142. Compare King James Version. See also Avraham Gileadi, *The Book of Isaiah: A New Translation with Interpretive Keys from the Book of Mormon* (Salt Lake City: Deseret Book, 1988), 206.

CHAPTER SOURCES

The chapters in this book have been drawn from the following sources:

"House of Glory," in Truman G. Madsen, *The Highest in Us* (Salt Lake City: Bookcraft, 1978), 93–107.

"Foundations of Temple Worship," BYU-Idaho devotional address, October 26, 2004.

"The Temple and the Mysteries of Godliness," condensed and revised from an address given under FARMS sponsorship in San Diego, California, October 1993.

"Blessings of the Temple," address given at the annual Law Society/Alumni Association dinner, October 28, 2004.

"House of Glory, House of Light, House of Love," in *May Christ Lift Thee Up: Talks from the 1998 Women's Conference Sponsored by Brigham Young University and the Relief Society* (Salt Lake City: Deseret Book, 1999), 314–39.

"Elijah and the Turning of Hearts," in Truman G. Madsen, *The Radiant Life* (Salt Lake City: Bookcraft, 1994), 105–15.

"Purposes of the Temple," in Stephen R. Covey and Truman G.

Madsen, *Marriage and Family: Gospel Insights* (Salt Lake City: Bookcraft, 1983), 41–50.

"Joseph Smith and the Kirtland Temple," in Truman G. Madsen, *Joseph Smith the Prophet* (Salt Lake City: Bookcraft, 1989), 67–82.

"Ancient Temples and the Restoration," in Truman Madsen, ed., *The Temple in Antiquity: Ancient Records and Modern Perspectives* (Provo, Utah: Brigham Young University, Religious Studies Center, 1984), 1–18.

"Putting On the Names: A Jewish-Christian Legacy," in John M. Lundquist and Stephen D. Ricks, eds., *By Study and Also By Faith: Essays in Honor of Hugh W. Nibley on the Occasion of His Eightieth Birthday* (Salt Lake City: Deseret Book and FARMS, 1990), 1:458–81.

INDEX